KW-068
Siberian Huskies

Front endpapers: *The Siberian Husky, a direct descendant of the eskimo dog bred by the semi-nomadic Chukchi people of northeastern Asia, is one of the finest sled dogs known to man. Photo, Robert Smith, Kent, England.*

Title page: *In the dog show world, Huskies are recognized in several colors. Owner, Janet Gryzlo. Photo, Isabelle Francais.*

Distributed in the UNITED STATES by T.F.H. Publications, Inc., One T.F.H. Plaza, Neptune City, NJ 07753; in CANADA to the Pet Trade by H & L Pet Supplies Inc., 27 Kingston Crescent, Kitchener, Ontario N2B 2T6; Rolf C. Hagen Ltd., 3225 Sartelon Street, Montreal 382 Quebec; in CANADA to the Book Trade by Macmillan of Canada (A Division of Canada Publishing Corporation), 164 Commander Boulevard, Agincourt, Ontario M1S 3C7; in ENGLAND by T.F.H. Publications Limited, Cliveden House/Priors Way/Bray, Maidenhead, Berkshire SL6 2HP, England; in AUSTRALIA AND THE SOUTH PACIFIC by T.F.H. (Australia) Pty. Ltd., Box 149, Brookvale 2100 N.S.W., Australia; in NEW ZEALAND by Ross Haines & Son, Ltd., 18 Monmouth Street, Grey Lynn, Auckland 2, New Zealand; in SINGAPORE AND MALAYSIA by MPH Distributors (S) Pte., Ltd., 601 Sims Drive, #03/07/21, Singapore 1438; in the PHILIPPINES by Bio-Research, 5 Lippay Street, San Lorenzo Village, Makati Rizal; in SOUTH AFRICA by Multipet Pty. Ltd., 30 Turners Avenue, Durban 4001. Published by T.F.H. Publications, Inc. Manufactured in the United States of America by T.F.H. Publications, Inc.

SIBERIAN HUSKIES

Beverly Pisano

With his steadfast devotion, eagerness to learn, and remarkable adaptability to all sorts of living conditions, the Siberian has served man in a number of capacities through the ages. Photo, Vincent Serbin.

Contents

History

Throughout man's history, the dog has served in a variety of roles—as hunter, companion, guardian, and worker. Early on, man came to depend on the dog for many things, and a bond developed between the two that has been continually reinforced throughout the ages.

Of all the dog breeds that have resulted from one common ancestor, the prehistoric Tomarctus, one stands alone as having served man the most in a number of capacities: the eskimo or sled dog. Today's Siberian Husky, Alaskan Malamute, and Samoyed are direct descendants of the eskimo dog. The eskimo dog classification was once comprised of different Arctic breeds, each serving an essential purpose for centuries in the frozen wilds of the Arctic and Antarctic regions—helping man survive against the cruel ravages of nature.

The eskimo tribes which utilized these dogs came to depend on them for many things: pulling heavy sledges for great distances over frozen tundra; drawing umiaks (boats made of animal skin); helping to secure game by assisting in the hunt; and, in the summers, carrying heavy loads as pack dogs.

Besides helping greatly in the day-to-day life and preservation of entire tribes of people, these hardy dogs also helped conquer previously uncharted lands.

Admiral Robert E. Peary of the United States Navy was assisted in his quest to find the North Pole by dogs who served in the helpful capacity of guide and sledge hauler. In Peary's expedition of 1893-95, he and his men were forced to turn around in defeat and head back for civilization. Peary eventually did reach his long dreamed of goal, and the role that the eskimo dogs played in his successful expedition must not be underestimated.

The eskimo dog appeared scattered in many places throughout its history, covering thousands of miles of territory in Siberia, Canada, Alaska, Greenland, Labrador, and Baffin Island. There has been some documentation to support the theory that at some time in the past, wolves were used in crossbreeding to the eskimos' dogs. A Dr. Edward Moffat Weyer, quoted in *Hutchinson's Dog Encyclopaedia* (an historic source of information), said: "It seems altogether likely that the dogs of the Eskimos have crossed to some extent with wolves. The skeletal similarity points to a relationship . . . I have never heard of an authentic

A medium-sized working dog, the Husky is naturally friendly and gentle in temperament. Photo, Isabelle Francais.

Each of these littermates has distinctive facial markings. Breeder, Elsa Marchesano of New York.

case of dogs and wolves interbreeding under natural conditions, but it seems quite likely."

Wolves were in fact trained at one time by some eskimo tribes for use as sled pullers. Despite any hopes the eskimos may have had for the wolves' working ability, they were found lacking as far as endurance goes. For overall excellence in the tasks of sledge-pulling and umiak-drawing, the eskimo dogs were by far the frontrunners.

It has been said that the Siberian Husky in particular derived its name from the eskimo tribes that were nicknamed "huskies" by the white men who made early expeditions to their lands. The "Siberian" in the name of the breed of course stems from the fact that the eskimo dog was originally found in Siberia, only to travel later with the eskimos across the Bering Strait on the way to Alaska.

The Siberian Husky as a distinct breed started to come

into prominence when Navy Rear
Admiral Richard E. Byrd took
with him, on a monumental
expedition, not the usual large
arctic breeds, but 50 or so of the
smaller dogs, the fleet-footed
Siberian Huskies. On this
expedition, Byrd hoped to sail
around the 16,000-mile coastline
of the continent of Antarctica.

*If you plan to go sledding with your
Siberian Husky, it is recommended
that you secure a strong, well-
balanced, durable, and flexible sled.
Photo by Vincent Serbin, courtesy of
Larry Freas.*

The 1933 expedition, called
Operation Highjump, employed
4000 men. After this historic
trek, it was decided by the
explorers that the husky-type
dog was by far the better one to
use, as the small size made for a
quicker dog. The Siberian Husky
was now on its way to becoming
the most popular dog to be used
in sled racing.

THE VALIANT RACE TO ALASKA

In 1925, there was an outbreak
of the dreaded diptheria in
Nome, Alaska. A savage, 80-
mile-an- hour blizzard prevented

any air travel at the time, so an alternate method of transporting serum to prevent the disease from spreading further had to be found. The nearest supply of serum was at Anchorage, Alaska, and it could be taken by Alaskan railroad, which operated throughout the winter, to Nenana. At Nenana, however, a virtual dead-end was encountered, as there was a rugged trail of over 600 miles yet to be traveled before Nome could be reached. The only way a catastrophic outbreak could be avoided, it seemed, was to have the serum driven up by relay dog sled teams. Tales of fortitude in the face of sub-zero temperatures and fierce snowstorms had long circulated about the eskimo dogs and their handlers, so this seemed a feasible method of transporting the precious serum. Gunnar Kasson led the first team of dogs to arrive in Nome on February 2, 1925. News of this heroic accomplishment was heralded throughout the world. The other men and dog teams involved in the "great serum run," as it was dubbed, also became prominent through a flurry of global newspaper accounts.

A great debt was owed, of course, to all of the dauntless dogs who made that historic run, but the name of one dog on that team stands alone in singular recognition. That is the name of

Balto, the lead dog who arrived in Nome with Gunnar Kasson. This dog had saved Kasson a number of times on this and other journeys, and as such he acquired the distinction of being Alaska's best lead dog.

In honor of this great dog's memory, a bronze statue of him was erected in Central Park in New York City, paying homage to this valiant veteran of countless

These are two of several types of harnesses used in sled-dog racing. Photo, Vincent Serbin.

arctic adventures, and to all others like him. The legend inscribed on the statue reads:

Dedicated to the indomitable spirit of the sled dogs that relayed antitoxin six hundred miles over rough ice, across treacherous waters, through arctic blizzards from Nenana to the relief of a stricken Nome in the winter of 1925. Endurance—fidelity—intelligence.

INSTRUMENTAL BREEDERS

The name of Leonhard Seppala is quite an important one in the history of the Siberian Husky. His kennel was located in Nome, where he used the Husky to race in competitions from 1909 to the mid 1920's. He was also involved in the "great serum run," after which he left Nome for Canada; he eventually settled in New England.

By far the most instrumental breeder in the US of the breed as became established here was Arthur Walden, who owned the Chinook Kennels of Wonalancet, New Hampshire. The Chinook Kennels are well known to just about everyone who is active in the Siberian Husky fancy. It was Walden who introduced two other avid fanciers to the breed, Milton Seeley and his wife Eva. The Husky stock that was the foundation of the Chinook kennels came directly from Alaska, and also from Leonhard Seppala's kennel.

A Swiss-style ski harness is worn by this Husky.

Once the Siberian Husky began receiving attention from important breeders, the road to total acceptance by the public was imminent. It did not take long for this breed to find its niche among the dog-loving and sporting-minded public, and it became a popular housepet, recreational and sled dog.

A Description of the Breed

With all that has been said and written about the Siberian Husky, one thing remains starkly obvious about members of the breed: each is unswervingly loyal to his master.

For ages, this brave and hearty worker has eagerly taken the command of his master. Whether he was being urged on into the uncharted frozen wilds of the Arctic and Antarctic regions or asked to haul heavy loads for long distances, the Siberian Husky took to the task with boundless energy.

Malamute. Once a Husky fancier, always a Husky fancier, the true lovers of the breed say, and this is borne out by the remarkable and ever-growing popularity of the breed.

HUSKY APPEARANCE

Perhaps the most striking feature of the Siberian Husky is the vivid blue eye color that is found in some specimens. And, while the blue eye color is prized by some breeders, the other colors that occur, such as brown or one brown with one blue, are

Such was the case with all the eskimo or sled dogs of old, and these attributes are still prized in the distinct arctic breeds that have developed through selective breeding: the Siberian Husky and the Alaskan

One doesn't need snow to race one's Siberians. Gig racing, using gigs (wheels) rather than sleds, has become quite popular. Photo, Vincent Serbin.

Above: *Most people who come face to face with a Siberian Husky are captivated by its striking beauty and sweet-natured expression. Photo, Isabelle Francais.*

Overleaf caption: *The moderately compact and well-furred body, the erect ears, and the brush tail suggest this handsome breed's Northern heritage. Photo, Isabelle Francais. Owner, B. Peterson.*

A Description of the Breed

attractive as well. Equally striking is the variety of coat patterns, in a wide range of colors: red and white, black and white, gray and white, and solid white. No two Siberian Huskies appear the same in regard to the pattern of coloration in the coat, and coloration can be very eye-catching and dramatic in certain specimens. A combination of crystal blue eyes and commanding coat pattern is a sure attention-getter at conformation shows.

The look of the Husky can be adequately described as strong and noble, and the way this breed moves is further illustration of nobility and gracefulness. The Husky appears to have great strength without compromising it at the expense of flowing carriage. In the show

Many people have the mistaken notion that all Siberian Huskies have blue eyes. According to the breed standard, the eyes can be brown also. Photo, Vincent Serbin.

ing, the Husky moves with graceful precision, and the ability to move in such a way is in fact demanded of show ring specimens.

The novice may find that the Husky is difficult to tell from the Alaskan Malamute, but on close inspection, it can be seen that the Malamute is a larger dog than the Husky. The average size for an Alaskan Malamute according to that breed's standard, is: males: 25 inches at the shoulder and 85 pounds; females: 23 inches at the shoulders and 75 pounds. For the Husky, males are 21 to 23½ inches at the withers (shoulders); and from 45 to 60 pounds; females are 20 to 22 inches and from 35 to 50 pounds.

Typically, a breed standard is drawn up by a national breed club (known as the parent club

Amid his many racing trophies is Silena's Lara, owned by Carol Rice of Massachusetts.

for that breed) and approved by the national kennel club, which is the governing body for all purebred dogs in a particular country. Any such standard is always subject to change through review by the national breed club. Standards may vary from country to country.

With regard to coat pattern, no two Siberian Huskies are alike. Photo, Isabelle Francais. Owner, Janet Gryzlo.

rooming

e Siberian Husky, with his
ort thick coat, will require a
nimum of grooming. Whereas
longhaired breeds such as the
ghan Hound, or a breed such
the Poodle, whose hair grows
pidly, frequent grooming is a
cessity, in the Siberian Husky
ere is little or no need to visit a
ooming parlor. Any grooming
at has to be done to your pet
n be accomplished in the
me, with little prior training.

The Husky has a double coat;
y that is meant that he has an
ndercoat that consists of soft,
ense hairs, and an outer coat
onsisting of guard hairs that are
arsh, giving the coat an even,
et never bristly, appearance.
he coat of the Husky is of
edium length, and the dog in
eneral appears well-furred.

Only a minimum of trimming
ill be required to neaten up the
iberian Husky's appearance
ow and then, to ready him for a
how ring appearance, or just for
e sake of having a well-
roomed dog of whom you can
e very proud. What will be more
me-consuming will be the
rushing that the dog will have to
ndergo, as this should ideally
e done at least twice a week.
his should not seem like too
uch of a chore to you, if you'll
top to consider the enormous
mount of time that goes into the
rooming of top show
pecimens who have long,
owing coats. The elegant Shih

Tzu and fluffy Old English
Sheepdogs that you see gaiting
before the judge at conformation
shows did not arrive at their
spectacular beauty naturally,
without having been worked on.
A good deal of patient work goes
into the grooming and priming of
a handsome, healthy dog.

If your Siberian Husky
receives the proper amounts of
love, attention, nutritious diet,
exercise, and has dry, clean
living quarters and periodic
health check-ups, the grooming
you give him will serve, so to

*Grooming the Siberian is simple and
includes clipping the nails with a pet
nail clipper. Photo, Vincent Serbin.*

speak, as the "icing on the cake." If your dog has the glow of a healthy, happy pet, a well-primed coat will only serve to further illustrate your care of and love for the dog.

BASIC TOOLS

For the grooming of your Siberian Husky, there are a number of tools that will have to be purchased at the outset. Usually, the best time to begin grooming sessions is when your Husky is still a pup, say from four months or so on up, so that he is easily acclimated to the procedure. You must remember the key word in any type of training that you want your new Siberian Husky to undergo: *patience.* This is especially important to remember for puppies. Your squirming Siberian pup will want to make a game of the grooming procedure at first, and he'll no doubt attempt to bite the brush and wiggle around on the table, making it next to impossible for you to do anything to him. If you are gentle yet firm with him, rewarding him with a treat and a kind pat every time he shows signs of learning to be still, you will begin to see definite and long-lasting results.

As youngsters mature, their markings become more definite. Photo, Isabelle Francais.

cause hair breakage. As well, a slicker, or stiff wire brush, will be required if your dog winds up with mats in his coat. Usually, a breed with a medium length coat such as the Husky is not as prone to mats as longer-haired breeds are, but occasionally you may find a tangle or two on inspection of the coat.

A steel comb will also be needed, as will a shedding blade,

Basic obedience training is important, and the sit-stay is one of the first lessons that your dog should master. Photo, Vincent Serbin.

To "stack" or "set up" a dog means to pose him so as to make the most of his appearance in the show ring. This Husky is in the process of being set up. Photo, Vincent Serbin.

Once you have decided to begin teaching your dog tolerance of the grooming program, you should visit your local pet shop for supplies. There will undoubtedly be a wide selection of grooming tools, from the basic to the advanced, for the novice and the professional. To begin with, you will need a good, natural bristle brush. A natural bristle brush is a far better choice than is a nylon one, because the former allows the coat's natural oils to be distributed evenly and does not

scissors, thinning shears, nail clipper, medicated ear powder, cotton, eye drops, and a coat conditioner containing lanolin.

To briefly explain the function and purpose of each of these items will help give you a better idea of the whole grooming process. The scissors will be used on the whiskers; the thinning shears on any unkempt hair growing between the toes and around the paws. The shedding blade will be required during the shedding seasons, which occur usually in the spring and in the fall, to remove dead hairs from the coat. The ear powder and eye drops, which your veterinarian can suggest or prescribe, are used to cleanse and soothe. Finally, the coat conditioner is applied directly onto the coat, where it works, when thoroughly rubbed in, to promote a healthy gloss. Of course, the healthiest sheen comes from within, so take advantage of the supplements that are available for inclusion with your dog's daily rations. If your dog is receiving a generally healthy diet, the good nutrition will most definitely show in his coat.

After all the materials have been purchased, and you have acquainted yourself with each item's use, it is time to look for a suitable area of the house in which to do the actual grooming. If you have a spare room,

Lovely head study of a black and white Husky. Note the almond-shaped eyes, moderately spaced and set at a slight oblique angle. The expression is keen but friendly. Photo, Vincent Serbin.

laundry room, or basement, one of these would be ideal, as they would offer ample space. If you don't wish to go for the expense of a grooming table, simply use any old table, first covering it with a rubberized slip-proof mat to ensure your dog's footing. Hopefully, the dog was trained to jump enthusiastically onto the table while he was still a pup, avoiding the problem of having to lift a large adult onto it!

Begin to brush the dog,

Grooming

working through the entire coat with firm, long strokes. If any mats are found, separate them first with your hands, then go through them with the slicker brush. If the hair is very badly matted, many groomers recommend soaking it first in almond oil, then separating each mat into three or four parts. From there, you can work the mat out from each section of hair you've separated, either with the fingers or the end tooth of a comb. Over-grooming of this breed, and especially excessive use of a comb, is not recommended, as it will remove the undercoat. A comb should be used only when the dog is shedding.

The nails are too long if they touch the ground when the dog walks, and they should be clipped at this time. It would be wise to have your vet show you the proper way to do this. It is important not to clip the nail too far down and hit the "quick." This is quite painful and can cause the nail to bleed. The nails will have to be clipped on the average of every two months or so, according to their rate of growth. A dog that is exercised a great deal on blacktop or hard surfaces has his nails worn down naturally. A housedog that runs in the yard or on dirt, however, will have to have his nails clipped periodically. Get in the habit of checking your Husky's nails

every six weeks or so.

Clean any mucous secretions that accumulate in the corners of your Husky's eyes with the eye drops and cotton. Again, on the suggestion of your vet, use whichever drops he recommends for the purpose. Place drops in each eye, applying them to the inside corner. Moisten the cotton with warm water, and wipe the corner of each eye and the underneath to remove any secretions.

The ears must be checked regularly for any accumulation of waxy secretions. After they've been inspected for and cleansed of wax or dirt, dust them with medicated powder.

For the Siberian Husky who will be shown, the epitome of perfect grooming is expected, so every little touch will be all the better in presenting him at his best. Such a touch is the clipping of the whiskers, with scissors. For the Siberian Husky who will be primarily a pet, and who won't undergo the scrutiny of the show judges, the whiskers can be left as is.

Facing page: *According to the breed standard, the Siberian Husky's ears are of medium size, triangular in shape, close fitting, and set high on the head. They are thick, well furred, slightly arched at the back, and strongly erect with slightly rounded tips pointing straight up. Photo, Isabelle Francais. Owner, Carolyn Duryea.*

Grooming

A six-foot training lead (above) is handy to have when teaching your Siberian Husky basic obedience commands. In the sit-stay command (below) the palm of one hand is placed in front of the dog while you say, "stay!" Photos, Vincent Serbin.

Any excess, unkempt hair that is growing between the paw pads can be trimmed to be even with the paw pads themselves. Use the thinning shears for this, taking care not to go down deeper than the surface of the pads. This is a very sensitive area of the dog's body, and a nick here can be painful and may even cause your dog to limp temporarily. The same can be done to any scraggly hairs growing between the toes, again cutting even with the outside edge of the paw and not going in between the toes.

After all of the de-matting, brushing, combing and clipping of hair and nails is achieved, you can bathe the dog. Keep in mind, though, that the Husky will require a minimum of bathing, as he is generally a clean dog whose coat usually appears neat and is free from doggy odor unless, of course, he has gotten into some foul-smelling substance or been playing in mud!

The water for your Husky's bath should be comfortably warm to your touch; never should it be too warm or too cold. Lukewarm is always the best temperature. Be sure to fill

Facing page: *The muzzle is of medium length, the stop well defined. Photo, Isabelle Francais. Owner, Janet Gryzlo.*

the tub or basin with enough water to allow the dog to be thoroughly soaked; it is important that his entire coat is wet. When it is thoroughly moistened, apply dog shampoo or soap, preferably one that contains conditioners, and work up a good lather. Be sure to lather each section of the body, including feet, tail and underside. Keep the suds out of his eyes and ears to prevent undue irritation. This can be accomplished by the application of a few drops of mineral oil into the eyes and cotton balls placed gently in the ears.

After a good enough lather has been worked into the dog's coat, give him his first rinse. There should be several rinses in all, to ensure that every bit of soap is removed from the coat. Always use clean water for the rinse; never use the dirty, sudsy water in the bottom of the tub.

Allow the excess water to drip off the dog for several moments before rubbing him with a thick terry towel. In warmer weather, the dog can be put out in the

If a dog becomes sick or injured during a dog sledding excursion, he should be wrapped in a "dog bag" so that he can be easily transported to safety. Photo, Vincent Serbin.

yard after being towel-dried.

After your Husky is completely dry, you may apply a lanolin-based coat conditioner to promote a healthy sheen. Rub a few drops of the conditioner into the coat, being sure to reach down to the skin. The massaging action of your hands, with their own natural oils, will also add to the sheen.

Huskies have been known to do well in obedience competition, as evidenced by this dog who scales the high jump.

The final product after all your efforts: a beautifully groomed and happy-looking Siberian Husky!

Selecting Your Dog

Now that you have decided which dog breed suits your needs, your lifestyle, and your own temperament, there will be much to consider before you make your final purchase. Buying a puppy on impulse may only cause heartbreak later on; it makes better sense to put some real thought into your canine investment, especially since it is likely that he will share many happy years with you. Which individual will you choose as your adoring companion? Ask yourself some questions as you analyze your needs and preferences for a dog, read all that you can about your particular breed, and visit as many dog shows as possible. At the shows you will be surrounded by people who can give you all the details about the breed you are interested in buying. Decide if you want a household pet, a dog for breeding, or a show dog. Would you prefer a male or female? Puppy or adult?

If you buy from a breeder, ask him to help you with your decision. When you have settled on the dog you want, discuss with him the dog's temperament, the animal's positive and negative aspects, any health problems it might have, its feeding and grooming requirements, and whether the dog has been immunized. Reputable breeders will be willing to answer any questions you might have that pertain to the dog you have selected, and often they will make themselves available if you call for advice or if you encounter problems after you've made your purchase.

Since Huskies are intelligent and learn quickly, it won't be difficult to teach them simple obedience commands such as the "stay." Photo, Vincent Serbin.

A bit too big?
A little **too** small.
Too fuzzy for me!
Too fat to crawl.

Before you wrap it tight
And crate it home,
Behold its appetite
And room to roam.

A sloppy yap, a barking slur,
Puppy eyes to be let free,
A him? a her? an unmarked cur,
Let's pout to see its pedigree.

The perfect pet quest:
Which pup for me is best?

ANDREW DE PRISCO

Selecting Your Dog

Most breeders want to see their dogs placed in loving, responsible homes; they are careful about who buys their animals. So as the dog's new owner, prepare yourself for some interrogation from the breeder.

WHERE TO BUY

You can choose among several places to buy your dog. One is a kennel whose business is breeding show-quality dogs but who also may have extra

In cold climates, Siberian Huskies are often the dog of choice.

pups for sale as pets. Another is the one-dog owner who wants to sell the puppies from an occasional litter to pay the expenses of his small-scale breeding operation. Pet shops usually buy puppies for re-sale from overstocked kennels or part-time hobbyists, and you can generally buy a puppy there at a reasonable price. To find any of these, check the classified section of your local newspaper or look in the Yellow Pages of your phone book. If you or your friends go driving out in the countryside, be on the lookout for a sign announcing purebred puppies for sale.

Whichever source you choose, you can usually tell in a very short time whether the puppies will make healthy and happy pets. If they are clean, plump, and lively, they are probably in good health. At the breeder's you will have the advantage of seeing the puppies' dam and perhaps their sire and other relatives. Remember that the mother, having just raised a demanding family, may not be looking her best; but if she is sturdy, friendly, and well-mannered, her puppies should be too. If you feel that something is lacking in the care or condition of the dogs, it is better to look elsewhere than to buy hastily and regret it afterward. Buy a healthy dog with a good disposition, one that has been

Dogs that are entered in weight-pulling contests are required to pull a load of 200 pounds a distance of 20 feet in 90 seconds in order to qualify for such events. Photo, Vincent Serbin.

properly socialized and likes being around people.

If you cannot find the dog you want locally, write to the secretary of the national breed club or kennel club and ask for names of breeders near you or to whom you can write for information. Puppies are often shipped, sight unseen, from reputable breeders. In these instances, pictures and pedigree information are usually sent beforehand to help you decide.

Breeders can supply you with further details and helpful guidance, if you require it. Many breed clubs provide a puppy referral service, so you may want to look into this before making your final decision.

PET OR SHOW DOG

Conscientious breeders strive to maintain those desirable qualities in their breed. At the same time, they are always working to improve on what they have already achieved, and they do this by referring to the breed standard of perfection. The standard describes the ideal dog, and those animals that come close to the ideal are generally selected as show

Owners of purebred dogs too often forget that all breeds of dog are interrelated. The ancient canine that is the believed ancestor of all dogs is known as Tomarctus. As packs traveled and inhabited various lands, types evolved through the process of adaptation. Later, as dogs and man joined forces, type became further diversified. This chart sketches one commonly accepted theory of the domesticated dog's development. Where does your dog fit in? With a few exceptions, dogs evolve or change as a result of a specific functional need.

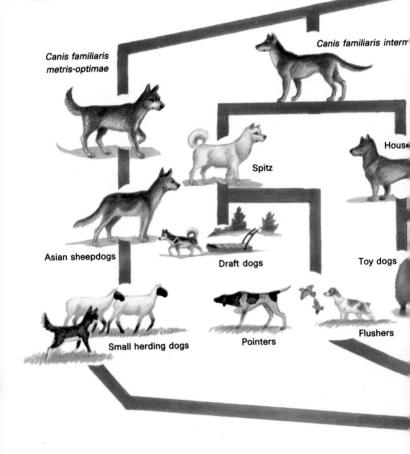

Canis familiaris intermⁱ

Canis familiaris metris-optimae

House

Spitz

Asian sheepdogs

Draft dogs

Toy dogs

Small herding dogs

Pointers

Flushers

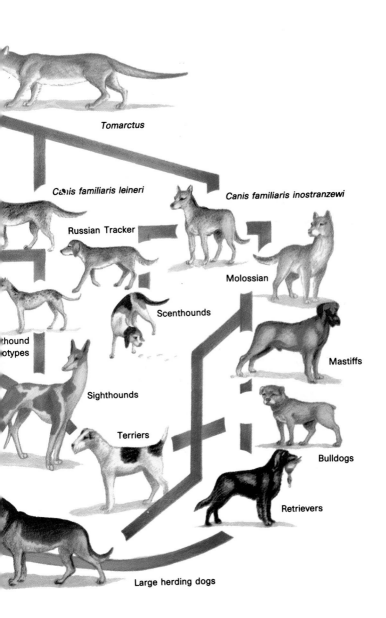

Tomarctus

Canis familiaris leineri

Canis familiaris inostranzewi

Russian Tracker

Molossian

Scenthounds

Mastiffs

hound
otypes

Sighthounds

Terriers

Bulldogs

Retrievers

Large herding dogs

stock; those that do not are culled and sold as pets. Keep in mind that pet-quality purebred dogs are in no way less healthy or attractive than show-quality specimens. It's just that the pet may have undesirable features (such as ears that are too large

Siberians make fine traveling companions. It is strongly recommended that you crate your dog, if possible, rather than allow him to ride unconfined in your vehicle. Photo, Vincent Serbin.

or eyes that are the wrong color for its breed) which would be faults in the show ring. Often these so-called "flaws" are detectable only by experienced breeders or show judges. Naturally the more perfect animal, in terms of its breed standard, will cost more—even though he seems almost identical to his pet-quality littermate.

If you think you may eventually want to show your dog or raise a litter of puppies, by all means buy the best you can afford. You will save expense and disappointment later on. However, if the puppy is strictly to be a pet for the children, or a companion for you, you can afford to look for a bargain. The pup which is not show material, or the older pup for which there is often less demand, or the grown dog which is not being used for breeding are occasionally available and offer opportunities to save money. Remember that your initial investment may be a bargain, but it takes good food and care— and plenty of both—to raise a healthy, vigorous puppy through its adulthood.

Facing page: *The healthy glow of this handsome Husky is evidence that he has been cared for properly. Photo, Isabelle Francais. Owner, Janet Gryzlo.*

The price you pay for your dog is little compared to the love and devotion he will return over the many years he'll be with you. With proper care and affection, your pup should live to a ripe old age; thanks to modern veterinary science and improvements in canine nutrition, dogs today are better maintained and live longer. It is not uncommon to see dogs living well into their teens.

Generally speaking, small dogs live longer than big ones. With love and the proper care any dog will live to its optimum age. Many persons, however,

opt for a particular breed because of its proven longevity. This, of course, is purely a personal decision.

MALE OR FEMALE

If you intend to breed your dog someday, by all means buy a female. You can find a suitable mate without difficulty when the time comes, and you'll have the pleasure of raising a litter of puppies. If you don't want to raise puppies, however, your female should be spayed so that she will remain a healthy, lively pet. Similarly, a male purchased as a pet, rather than as a stud

This illustration of the dog's skeleton and vital organs reveals the distinctive construction of the dog. Veterinary medicine, largely devoted to the better health of your dog, continues to make advances that promise even greater canine longevity.

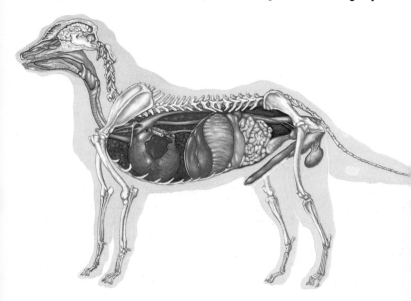

According to some astrologers, dogs too are affected by their zodiac sign. If you follow the stars, be sure to select a dog born under a sky compatible with that of your birth date.

dog, should be castrated. The female is smaller than the male and generally quieter. She has less tendency to roam in search of romance, but a properly trained male can be a charming pet and has a certain difference in temperament that is appealing to many people. Male versus female is chiefly a matter of personal choice; both make fine companions.

ADULT OR PUP

Whether to buy a grown dog or a young puppy is another question. It is surely an undeniable pleasure to watch your dog grow from a lively pup to a mature, dignified dog. If you don't have the time to spend on the more frequent meals, housebreaking, and other training a puppy needs in order to become a dog you can be proud of, then choose an older, partly-trained adolescent or a grown dog. If you want a show dog, remember that no one, not even an expert, can predict with one hundred percent accuracy what a puppy will be like when he grows up. The dog may seem to exhibit show potential *most* of the time, but six months is the earliest age for the would-be exhibitor to select a prospect and know that its future is in the show ring.

If you have a small child, it is best to get a puppy big enough to defend itself, one not less than four or five months old.

Older children will enjoy playing with and helping to take care of a baby pup; but at less than four months, a puppy wants to do little else but eat and sleep, and he must be protected from teasing and overtiring. You cannot expect a very young child to understand that a puppy is a fragile living being; to the youngster he is a toy like his

Winning the Working Group for owner Marie Wamser of Connecticut is American, Bermudian, and Canadian Champion Fra-Mar's Soan Diavol.

Polyurethane Flexible Floppy Flying Discs

The greatest advance in flying discs came with the manufacture of these discs from polyurethane. The polyurethane is so soft that it doesn't hurt you, your dog, or the window it might strike accidentally. Only very, very rarely can it break a window—usually one that was already cracked. The polyurethane Gumadisc® is floppy and soft. It can be folded

Gumabone® flying discs are proven safe and durable for dogs. The soft, pliable texture and the scent impregnation make these discs loved by dogs.

and fits into your pocket. It is also much tougher than cheap plastics, and most pet shops guarantee that it will last ten times longer than cheap plastic discs.

With most flying discs made for dogs comes an instruction booklet on how to use the disc with your canine friend. Basically, you play with the dog and the disc so the dog knows the disc belongs to him. Then you throw it continuously, increasing the distance, so that the dog fetches it and brings it back to you.

The exercise for you comes in when your dog stops fetching it, or when you have a partner. The two of you play catch. You stand as far apart as available space allows—usually 30–35 m (100 feet) is more than enough room. You throw the disc to each other, arousing your dog's interest as he tries to catch it. When the disc is dropped or veers off, the dog grabs it and brings it back (hopefully). Obviously you will have to run to catch the disc before your dog does.

There are contests held all over the world where distance, height, and other characteristics are measured competitively. Ask your local pet shop to help you locate a Frisbee® Club near you.

*Frisbee® is a trademark of the Kransco Company, California, and is used for their brand of flying disc.

In preparation for the show ring, a dog must learn to gait at his owner's side. Photo, Vincent Serbin.

stuffed dog. Children, therefore, must learn how to handle and care for their young pets.

We recommend you start with a puppy so that you can raise and train it according to the rules you have established in your own home. While a dog is young, its behavior can be more easily shaped by the owner, whereas an older dog , although trainable, may be a bit set in his ways.

WHAT TO LOOK FOR IN A PUPPY

In choosing a puppy, assuming that it comes from healthy, well-bred parents, look for one that is friendly and outgoing. The biggest pup in the litter is apt to be somewhat coarse as a grown dog, while the appealing "runt of the litter" may turn out to be a timid shadow—or have a Napoleonic complex! If you want a show dog and have no experience in choosing a prospect, study the breed standard and listen carefully to the breeder on the finer points of show conformation. A breeder's prices will be in accord with his puppies' expected worth, and he will be honest with you about each pup's potential because it is to his own advantage. He wants his top-quality show puppies placed in the public eye to reflect glory on him—and to attract future buyers. Why should he sell a potential show champion to someone who just wants a pet?

Now that you have paid your money and made your choice, you are ready to depart with puppy, papers, and instructions. Make sure that you know the youngster's feeding routine, and take along some of his food. For the trip home, place him in a comfortable, sturdy carrier. Do not drive home with a puppy on your lap! If you'll be travelling for a few hours, at the very least bring along a bottle of water from the breeder and a small water dish.

PEDIGREE AND REGISTRATION

Owners of puppies are often misled by sellers with such ruses as leading the owner to believe his dog is something special. The term *pedigree papers* is quite different from the term *registration papers*. A pedigree is nothing more than a statement made by the breeder of the dog;

Dog shows are fascinating to both the participants and the spectators. If you have never attended a dog show, you are missing an important part of the canine world. This is the Crufts Show in England.

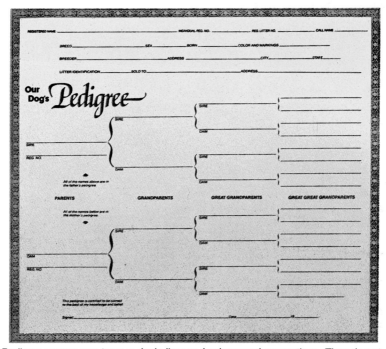

Pedigree papers can trace a dog's lineage back several generations. They do not, however, guarantee that a puppy is of good quality or sound health.

and it is written on special pedigree blanks, which are readily available from any pet shop or breed club, with the names of several generations from which the new puppy comes. It records your puppy's ancestry and other important data, such as the pup's date of birth, its breed, its sex, its sire and dam, its breeder's name and address, and so on. If your dog has had purebred champions in his background, then the pedigree papers are valuable as evidence of the good breeding behind your dog; but if the names on the pedigree paper are meaningless, then so is the paper itself. Just because a dog has a pedigree doesn't necessarily mean he is registered with a kennel club.

Registration papers from the American Kennel Club or the United Kennel Club in the United States or The Kennel Club of Great Britain attest to the fact that the mother and father of your puppy were purebred dogs of the breed represented by your puppy and that they were registered with a particular club. Normally every registered dog also has a complete pedigree available. Registration papers, which you receive when you buy a puppy, merely enable you to register your puppy. Usually the breeder has registered only the litter, so it is the new owner's responsibility to register and name an individual pup. The papers should be filled out and sent to the appropriate address printed on the application, along with the fee required for the registration. A certificate of registration will then be sent to you.

Pedigree and registration, by the way, have nothing to do with licensing, which is a local regulation applying to purebred and mongrel alike. Find out what the local ordinance is in your town or city and how it applies to your dog; then buy a license and keep it on your dog's collar for identification.

A Husky from the Kaylee Kennels of Carolyn Windsor.

n this breed, the neck should be medium in length, arched, and carried proudly erect when the dog is standing. A neck that is too short and thick or one that is too long is considered a fault in the show ring. Photo, Isabelle Francais.

At long last, the day you have all been waiting for, your new puppy will make its grand entrance into your home. Before you bring your companion to its new residence, however, you must plan carefully for its arrival. Keep in mind that the puppy will need time to adjust to life with a different owner. He may seem a bit apprehensive about the strange surroundings in which he finds himself, having spent the first few weeks of life with his dam and littermates, but in a couple of days, with love and patience on your part, the transition will be complete.

First impressions are important, especially from the puppy's point of view, and these may very well set the pattern of his future relationship with you. You must be consistent in the

A crate, for home and travel, is standard equipment and makes an excellent gift for the new dog owner.

way you handle your pet so that he learns what is expected of him. He must come to trust and respect you as his keeper and master. Provide him with proper care and attention, and you will be rewarded with a loyal companion for many years. Considering the needs of your puppy and planning ahead will surely make the change from his former home to his new one easier.

ADVANCE PREPARATION

In preparing for your puppy's arrival, perhaps more important than anything else is to find out from the seller how the pup was maintained. What brand of food was offered and when and how often was the puppy fed? Has

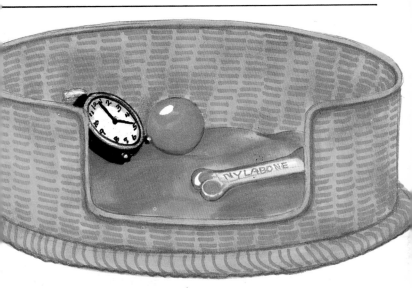

A warm bed, equipped with a ticking clock, chew bone, and safe dog toy, can help a pup feel secure and welcome in its new home.

he pup been housebroken; if so, what method was employed? Attempt to continue whatever routine was started by the person from whom you bought your puppy; then, gradually, you can make those changes that suit you and your lifestyle. If, for example, the puppy has been paper trained, plan to stock up on newspaper. Place this newspaper toilet facility in a selected spot so that your puppy learns to use the designated area as his "bathroom." And keep on hand a supply of the dog food to which he is accustomed, as a sudden switch to new food could cause digestive upsets.

Another consideration is sleeping and resting quarters. Be sure to supply a dog bed for your pup, and introduce him to his special cozy corner so that he knows where to retire when he feels like taking a snooze. You'll need to buy a collar (or harness) and leash, a safe chew item (such as Nylabone® or Gumabone®), and a few grooming tools as well. A couple of sturdy feeding dishes, one for food and one for water, will be needed; and it will be necessary, beforehand, to set up a feeding station.

FINDING A VETERINARIAN

An important part of your preparations should include finding a local veterinarian who can provide quality health care in the form of routine check-ups, inoculations, and prompt medical attention in case of illness or an emergency. Find out if the animal you have selected has been vaccinated against canine diseases, and make certain you secure all health certificates at the time of purchase. This information will be valuable to your veterinarian, who will want to know the puppy's complete medical history. Incidentally, don't wait until your puppy becomes sick before you seek the services of a vet; make an appointment for your pup before or soon after he takes up residence with you so that he starts out with a clean bill of health in his new home.

CHILDREN AND PUPPIES

Prepare the young members of the household on pet care. Children should learn not only to love their charges but to respect them and treat them with the consideration one would give all living things. It must be emphasized to youngsters that the puppy has certain needs, just as humans have, and all family members must take an active role in ensuring that these needs are met. Someone must feed the puppy. Someone must walk him a couple of times a day or clean up after him if he is trained to relieve himself on newspaper. Someone must groom his coat, clean his ears, and clip his nails from time to time. Someone

must see to it that the puppy gets sufficient exercise and attention each day.

A child who has a pet to care for learns responsibility; nonetheless, parental guidance is an essential part of his learning experience. Many a child has been known to "love a pet to death," squeezing and hugging the animal in ways which are irritating or even painful. Others have been found guilty of teasing, perhaps unintentionally, and disturbing their pet while the animal is eating or resting. One must teach a child, therefore, when and how to gently stroke and fondle a puppy. In time, the child can learn how to carefully pick up and handle the pup. A dog should always be supported with both hands, *not* lifted by the scruff of the neck. One hand placed under the chest, between the front legs, and the other hand supporting the dog's rear end will be comfortable and will restrain the animal as you hold and carry him. Always demonstrate to children the proper way to lift a dog.

BE A GOOD NEIGHBOR

For the sake of your dog's safety and well being, don't allow him to wander onto the property of others. Keep him confined at all times to your own yard or indoors where he won't become a nuisance. Consider what

If you purchase a Siberian Husky puppy from a reputable breeder, chances are that you will be able to see its sire or dam. Photo, Isabelle Francais. Owner, Carolyn Duryea.

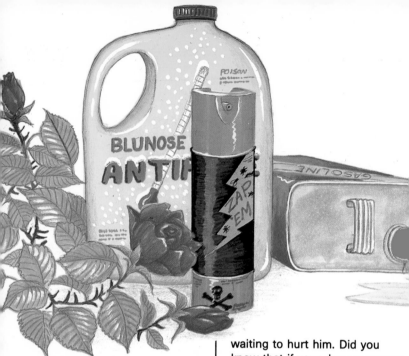

Many dangers lurk around the house. Keep all poisonous substances and sharp objects away from your curious pup.

dangers lie ahead for an unleashed dog that has total freedom of the great outdoors, particularly when he is unsupervised by his master. There are cars and trucks to dodge on the streets and highways. There are stray animals with which to wrangle. There are poisons all around, such as car antifreeze in driveways or toxic plants and shrubs, which, if swallowed, could prove fatal. There are dognappers and sadistic people who may steal or bring harm to your beloved pet. In short, there are all sorts of nasty things

waiting to hurt him. Did you know that if your dog consumes rotting garbage, there is the possibility he could go into shock or even die? And are you aware that a dog left to roam in a wooded area or field could become infected with any number of parasites if he plays with or ingests some small prey, such as a rabbit, that might be carrying these parasitic organisms? A thorn from a rosebush imbedded in the dog's foot pad, tar from a newly paved road stuck to his coat, and a wound inflicted by a wild animal all can be avoided if you take the precaution of keeping your dog in a safe enclosure where he will be protected from such dangers. Don't let your dog run loose; he is likely to stray from home and get into all sorts of trouble.

Clockwise from upper right: *pokeweed, jimson weed, foxglove, and yew.* If ingested, a toxic plant can be dangerous to your dog.

The New Family Member

GETTING ACQUAINTED

Plan to bring your new pet home in the morning so that by nightfall he will have had some time to become acquainted with you and his new environment. Avoid introducing the pup to the family around holiday time, since all of the extra excitement will only add to the confusion and frighten him. Let the puppy enter your home on a day when the

Resist the temptation to handle him too much during these first few days. And, if there are other dogs or animals around the house, make certain all are properly introduced. If you observe fighting among the animals, or some other problem, you may have to separate all parties until they learn to accept one another. Remember that neglecting your other pets while

routine is normal. For those people who work during the week, a Saturday morning is an ideal time to bring the puppy to his new home; this way he has the entire weekend to make adjustments before being left alone for a few hours, come Monday morning.

Let the puppy explore, under your watchful eye of course, and let him come to know his new home without stress and fear.

A team of Huskies, belonging to Mrs. Lorna Demidoff, takes a short break on the snow-covered grounds of New Hampshire.

Facing page: *The Fischers of Pennsylvania own these two gorgeous dogs, Champion Monadnock's Misty of Arahaz and Monadnock's Mischa of Arahaz.*

showering the new puppy with extra attention will only cause animosity and jealousy. Make an effort to pay special attention to the other animals as well.

On that eventful first night, try not to give in and let the puppy sleep with you; otherwise, this could become a difficult habit to break. Let him cry and whimper, even if it means a night of restlessness for the entire family. Some people have had success with putting a doll or a hot water bottle wrapped in a towel in the puppy's bed as a surrogate mother, while others have placed a ticking alarm clock in the bed to simulate the heartbeat of the pup's dam and littermates. Remember that this furry little fellow is used to the warmth and security of his mother and siblings, so the adjustment to sleeping alone will take time. Select a location away from drafts and away from the feeding station for placement of his dog bed. Keep in mind, also, that the bed should be roomy enough for him to stretch out in; as he grows older, you may need to supply a larger one.

Prior to the pup's arrival, set up his room and partition it the way you would to keep an infant out of a particular area. You may want to keep his bed, his feeding station, and his toilet area all in the same room—in separate locations—or you may want to set the feeding station up in your kitchen, where meals for all family members are served. Whatever you decide, do it ahead of time so you will have that much less to worry about when your puppy finally moves in with you.

Above all else, be patient with your puppy as he adjusts to life in his new home. If you purchase a pup that is not housebroken, you will have to spend time with the dog—just as you would with a small child—until he develops proper toilet habits. Even a housebroken puppy may feel nervous in strange new surroundings and have an occasional accident. Praise and encouragement will elicit far better results than punishment or scolding. Remember that your puppy wants nothing more than to please you, thus he is anxious to learn the behavior that is required of him.

Feeding Requirements

Perhaps more than any other single aspect of your dog's development, proper feeding requires an educated and responsible dog owner. The importance of nutrition on your dog's bone and muscle growth cannot be over emphasized.

Soon after your puppy comes to live with you, he will need to be fed. Remember to ask the seller what foods were given to the youngster and stay with that diet for a while. It is important for the puppy to keep eating and to avoid skipping a meal, so entice him with the food to which he is accustomed. If you prefer to switch to some other brand of dog food, each day begin to add small quantities of the new brand to the usual food offering. Make the portions of the new food progressively larger until the pup is weaned from his former diet.

What should you feed the puppy and how often? His diet is really quite simple and relatively inexpensive to prepare. Puppies need to be fed small portions at frequent intervals, since they are growing and their activity level is high. You must ensure that your pup gains weight steadily; with an adult dog, however, growth slows down and weight must be regulated to prevent obesity and a host of other problems. At one time, it was thought that home-cooked meals were the answer, with daily rations of meat,

The canine digestive system is adapted for omnivorous eating habits. Canines require both animal and vegetable matter for good health.

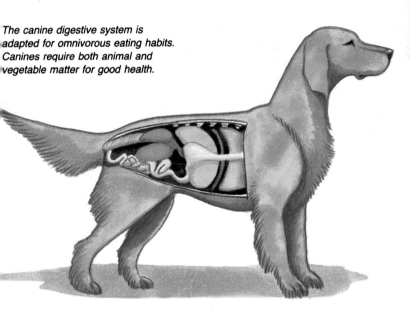

Feeding Requirements

vegetables, egg yolk, cereal, cheese, brewer's yeast, and vitamin supplements. With all of the nutritionally complete commercial dog food products readily available, these time-consuming preparations really are unnecessary now. A great deal of money and research has resulted in foods that we can serve our dogs with confidence and pride; and most of these commercial foods have been developed along strict guidelines according to the size, weight, and age of your dog. These products are reasonably priced, easy to find, and convenient to store.

THE PUPPY'S MEALS

After a puppy has been fully weaned from its mother until approximately three months of age, it needs to be fed four times a day. In the morning and evening offer kibble (dog meal) soaked in hot water or broth, to which you have added some canned meat-based food or fresh raw meat cut into small chunks. At noon and bedtime feed him a bit of kibble or whole-grain cereal moistened with milk (moistening, by the way, makes the food easier to digest, since dogs don't typically chew their food). From three to six months, increase the portion size and

A basketful of cute puppies, each one ready to go to its new home. Photo, Judy Rosemarin.

ire crates, such as these, are a ife means of confinement for your berian Husky. On long trips, let ur dog out of the crate to get some ercise. Photo, Vincent Serbin.

fer just three meals—one milk d two meat. At six months, o meals are sufficient; at one ar, a single meal can be given, pplemented with a few dry scuits in the morning and ening. During the colder onths, especially if your dog is ctive, you might want to mix in me wheat germ oil or corn oil bacon drippings with the meal add extra calories. Remember keep a bowl of cool, fresh ater on hand always to help ur dog regulate its body mperature and to aid in gestion.

From one year on, you may continue feeding the mature dog a single meal (in the evening, perhaps, when you have your supper), or you may prefer to divide this meal in two, offering half in the morning and the other half at night. Keep in mind that while puppies require foods in small chunks, or nuggets, older dogs can handle larger pieces of food at mealtime. Discuss your dog's feeding schedule with your veterinarian; he can make suggestions about the right diet for your particular canine friend.

COMPARISON SHOPPING

With so many fine dog-food products on the market today, there is something for

Feeding Requirements

everyone's pet. You may want to serve dry food "as is" or mix it with warm water or broth. Perhaps you'll choose to combine dry food with fresh or canned preparations. Some canned foods contain all meat, but they are not complete; others are mixtures of meat and grains, which have been fortified with additional nutrients to make them more complete and balanced. There are also various packaged foods that can be served alone or as supplements and that can be left out for a fe hours without spoiling. This se feeding method, which works well for dogs that are not pron to weight problems, allows the animal to serve himself whenever he feels hungry. Mar people who work during the da find these dry or semi-moist rations convenient to use, and these foods are great to bring along if you travel with your do

Be sure to read the labels carefully before you make your dog-food purchases. Most

Pet shops offer a large selection of quality bowls that are efficient and affordab. Offered in a wide variety of colors, bowls are easy to coordinate.

getables, grains, meats and dairy products are all vital components of ur dog's diet. Fortunately, mmercial dog foods are nutritionally lanced and easily digestible.

putable pet-food anufacturers list the gredients and the nutritional ntent right on the can or ckage. Instructions are usually cluded so that you will know w much to feed your dog to ep him thriving and in top ndition. A varied, well-lanced diet that supplies the

proper amounts of protein, carbohydrate, fat, vitamins, minerals, and water is important to keep your puppy healthy and to guarantee his normal development. Adjustments to the diet can be made, under your veterinarian's supervision, according to the individual puppy, his rate of growth, his activity level, and so on. Liquid or powder vitamin and mineral supplements, or those in tablet form, are available and can be given if you need to feel certain that the diet is balanced.

Siberian pups, like these, can be purchased from reputable breeders or from reputable pet shops. Before making your final selection, visit several sources and ask many questions of each prospective seller. Photo, Isabelle Francais. Owner, Carolyn Duryea.

DEVELOPING GOOD EATING HABITS

Try to serve your puppy his meals at the same time each day and in the same location so that he will get used to his daily routine and develop good eating habits. A bit of raw egg, cottage cheese, or table scraps (leftover food from your own meals) can be offered from time to time; but never accustom your dog to eating human "junk food." Cake, candy, chocolate, soda, and other snack foods are for people, not dogs. Besides, these foods provide only "empty" calories that your pet doesn't need if he is to stay healthy. Avoid offering spicy, fried, fatty, or starchy foods; rather, offer leftover meats, vegetables, and gravies. Get in the habit of feeding your puppy or your grown dog his *own* daily meals of dog food. If ever you are in doubt about what foods and how much to serve, consult your veterinarian.

Feeding your dog need not be a messy chore, provided that non-tipping, easy-clean bowls are used for each meal.

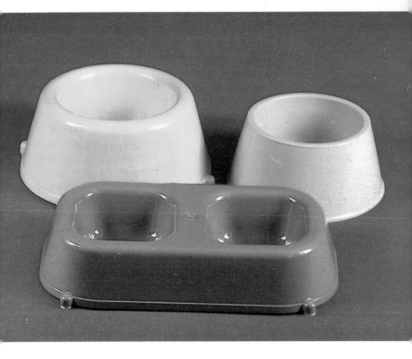

Feeding Requirements

FEEDING GUIDELINES

Some things to bear in mind with regard to your dog's feeding regimen follow.

- Nutritional balance, provided by many commercial dog foods, is vital; avoid feeding a one-sided all-meat diet. Variety in the kinds of meat (beef, lamb, chicken, liver) or cereal grains (wheat, oats, corn) that you offer your dog is of secondary importance compared to the balance or "completeness" of dietary components.
- Always refrigerate opened canned food so that it doesn't spoil. Remember to remove all uneaten portions of canned or moistened food from the feeding dish as soon as the pup has finished his meal. Discard the leftover food immediately and thoroughly wash and dry the feeding dish, as a dirty dish is a breeding ground for harmful germs.
- When offering dry foods, always keep a supply of water on hand for your dog. Water should be made available at all times, even if dry foods are not left out for self-feeding. Each day the water dish should be washed with soap and hot water, rinsed well, and dried; a refill of clean, fresh water should be provided daily.
- Food and water should be served at room temperature, neither too hot nor too cold, so that it is more palatable for your puppy.
- Serve your pup's meals in sturdy hard-plastic, stainless steel, or earthenware containers, ones that won't tip over as the dog gulps his food down. Some bowls and dishes are weighted to prevent spillage, while others fit neatly into holders which offer support. Feeding dishes should be large enough to hold each meal.
- Whenever the nutritional needs of your dog change— that is to say, when it grows older or if it becomes ill, obese, or pregnant; or if it starts to nurse its young— special diets are in order. Always contact your vet for advice on these special dietary requirements.
- Feed your puppy at the same regular intervals each day; reserve treats for special occasions or, perhaps, to reward good behavior during training sessions.
- Hard foods, such as biscuits and dog meal, should be offered regularly. Chewing on these hard, dry morsels helps the dog keep its teeth clean and its gums conditioned.
- Never overfeed your dog. If given the chance, he will accept and relish every in-between-meal tidbit you offer him. This pampering will only put extra weight on your pet

Made from 89% digestible cheese protein, this Chooz™ treat is purported to be the most healthy dog chew available. If it's too hard for your dog, simply microwave it for a minute or so and it becomes a crispy, crunchy, delectable dog biscuit. It comes in many sizes.

and cause him to be unhealthy in the long run.

- Do not encourage your dog to beg for food from the table while you are eating your meals.

- Food can be effectively used by the owner to train the dog. Doggie treats are practical and often nutritional—choose your chew treats choosily.

FEEDING CHART

Age and No. of Feedings Per Day	Weight in Lbs.	Weight in Kg.	Caloric Requirement kcal M.E./Day
Puppies—Weaning to 3 months Four per day	1–3	.5–1.4	124–334
	3–6	1.4–2.7	334–574
	6–12	2.7–5.4	574–943
	12–20	5.4–9.1	943–1384
	15–30	6.8–13.6	1113–1872
Puppies—3 to 6 months Three per day	3–10	1.4–4.5	334–816
	5–15	2.3–6.8	494–1113
	12–25	5.4–11.3	943–1645
	20–40	9.1–18.2	1384–2352
	30–70	13.6–31.8	1872–3542
Puppies—6 to 12 months Two per day	6–12	2.7–5.4	574–943
	12–25	5.4–11.3	943–1645
	20–50	9.1–22.7	1384–2750
	40–70	18.2–31.8	2352–3542
	70–100	31.8–45.4	3542–4640
Normally Active Adults One or two per day	6–12	2.7–5.4	286–472
	12–25	5.4–11.3	472–823
	25–50	11.3–22.7	823–1375
	50–90	22.7–40.8	1375–2151
	90–175	40.8–79.4	2151–3675

This chart presents general parameters of a dog's caloric requirements, based on weight. The total caloric intake comes from a complete, balanced diet of quality foods. To assist owners, dog food companies generally provide the nutritional information of their product right on the label.

Accommodations

Puppies newly weaned from their mother and siblings should be kept warm at all times. As they get older, they can be acclimated gradually to cooler temperatures. When you purchase your dog, find out from the seller whether he is hardy and can withstand the rigors of outdoor living. Many breeds have been known to adapt well to a surprising number of

invest in a crate for him to call his "home" whenever he needs to be confined for short intervals. You might plan to partition off a special room, or part of a room, for your pooch; or you may find that a heated garage or finished basement works well as your dog's living quarters. If your breed can tolerate living outside, you may want to buy or build him his own dog house with an

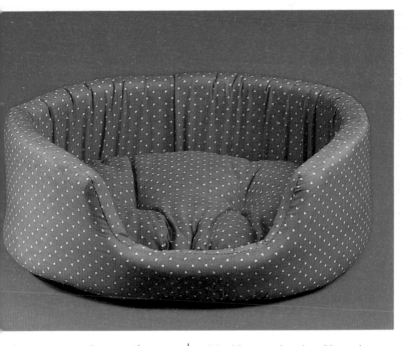

environments, so long as they are given time to adjust. If your pup is to be an indoor companion, perhaps a dog bed in the corner of the family room will suffice; or you may want to

A bed for your dog gives him a place to call his own. His bed should be placed in a warm, dry, draft-free location.

Accommodations

attached run. It might be feasible to place his house in your fenced-in backyard. The breed that can live outdoors fares well when given access to some sort of warm, dry shelter during periods of inclement weather. As you begin thinking about where your canine friend will spend most of his time, you'll want to consider his breed, his age, his temperament, his need for exercise, and the money, space, and resources you have available to house him.

THE DOG BED

In preparing for your puppy's arrival, it is recommended that dog bed be waiting for him so that he has a place to sleep and rest. If you have provided him with his own bed or basket, ensure that it is placed in a warm, dry, draft-free spot that i private but at the same time nea the center of family activity. Refrain from placing his bed nea the feed and water dishes or hi toilet area. You may want to giv your puppy something with

Dog beds come in a variety of sizes and styles and are easily acquired at your loca pet shop. Choose one that will accommodate your puppy when he has reached hi full-grown size.

Use discretion when giving your dog a toy. Children's toys are not puppies' toys. A pup can easily remove and ingest a button-eye, causing serious complications and even death.

which to snuggle, such as a laundered towel or blanket or an article of old clothing. Some dogs have been known to chew apart their beds and bedding, but you can easily channel this chewing energy into more constructive behavior simply by supplying him with some safe toys or a Nylabone® pacifier for

gnawing. Pet shops stock dog beds, among other supplies that you might need for your pup. Select a bed that is roomy, comfortable, and easy to clean, keeping in mind that you may have to replace the smaller bed with a larger one as the puppy grows to adulthood. Remember to clean and disinfect the bed and sleeping area from time to time, as these can become parasitic playgrounds for fleas, lice, mites, and the like.

Accommodations

THE CRATE

Although many dog lovers may cringe at the mere mention of the word *crate,* thinking of it as a cage or a cruel means of confinement, this handy piece of equipment can be put to good use for puppies and grown dogs alike. Even though you may love your dog to an extraordinary degree, you may not want him to have free rein of the house, particularly when you are not home to supervise him. If used properly, a crate can restrict your dog when it is not convenient to have him underfoot, *i.e.,* when guests are visiting or during your mealtimes.

A surprising number of dog owners, who originally had negative feelings about crating their dogs, have had great success using crates. The crate itself serves as a bed, provided it is furnished with bedding material, or it can be used as an indoor dog house. Not all dogs readily accept crates or being confined in them for short intervals, so for these dogs, another means of restriction must be found. But for those dogs that do adjust to spending

Crates allow for safe and easy travel and aid in the housebreaking process. Crates come in a variety of sizes, styles and colors.

me in these structures, the crate can be useful in many ways. The animal can be confined for a few hours while you are away from home or at work, or you can bring your crated dog along with you in the car when you travel or go on vacation. Crates also prove handy as carriers whenever you have to transport a sick dog to the veterinarian.

Most crates are made of sturdy wire or plastic, and some of the collapsible models can be conveniently stored or folded so that they can be moved easily from room to room or from inside the house to the yard on a warm, sunny day. If you allow your puppy or grown dog to become acquainted with its crate by cleverly propping the door open and leaving some of his favorite toys inside, in no time he will come to regard the crate as his own doggie haven. As with a dog bed, place the crate away from drafts in a dry, warm spot; refrain from placing food and water dishes in it, as these only crowd the space and offer opportunity for spillage.

If you need to confine your puppy so that he can't get into mischief while you're not home, remember to consider the animal's needs at all times. Select a large crate, one in which the dog can stand up and move around comfortably; in fact, bigger is better in this context.

The crate you choose for your dog should be appropriately sized. A crate can provide the new pet with a sense of security and belonging. Easily accessible, crates are an inexpensive, sensible investment.

Never leave the animal confined for more than a few hours at a time without letting him out to exercise, play, and, if necessary, relieve himself. Never crate a dog for ten hours, for example, unless you keep the door to the crate open so that he can get out for food and water and to stretch a bit. If long intervals of confinement are necessary, consider placing the unlatched crate in a partitioned section of your house or apartment.

Crates have become the answer for many a dog owner faced with the dilemma of either

Accommodations

getting rid of a destructive dog or living with him despite his bad habits. People who have neither the time nor the patience to train their dogs, or to modify undesirable behavior patterns, can at least restrain their pets during the times they can't be there to supervise. So long as the crate is used in a humane fashion, whereby a dog is confined for no more than a few hours at any one time, it can figure importantly in a dog owner's life. Show dogs, incidentally, learn at an early age that much time will be spent in and out of crates while they are on the show circuit. Many canine celebrities are kept in their crates until they are called to ringside, and they spend many hours crated to and from the shows.

THE DOG HOUSE

These structures, often made of wood, should be sturdy and

Consider your dog's present and fully grown size before purchasing the proper crate for him.

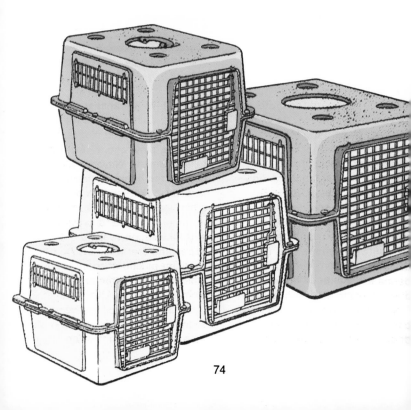

Commercial dog houses are designed for comfort and pest control.

offer enough room for your dog to stretch out in when it rests or sleeps. Dog houses that are elevated or situated on a platform protect the animal from cold and dampness that may seep through the ground. Of the breeds that are temperature hardy and will live outdoors, some are housed outside during the daytime only; others are permanent outdoor residents day and night, all year 'round.

If your intention is to have a companion that lives out-of-doors, it will be necessary to provide him with a more elaborate house, one that really protects him from the elements. Make sure the dog's house is constructed of waterproof materials. Furnish him with sufficient bedding to burrow into on a chilly night and provide extra insulation to keep out drafts and wet weather. Add a partition (a kind of room divider which separates the entry area from the main sleeping space) inside his house or attach a swinging door to the entrance to help keep him warm when he is

Accommodations

inside his residence. The swinging door facilitates entry to and from the dog house, while at the same time it provides protection, particularly from wind and drafts.

Some fortunate owners whose yards are enclosed by high fencing allow their dogs complete freedom within the boundaries of their property. In these situations, a dog can leave his dog house and get all the exercise he wants. Of course such a large space requires more effort to keep it clean. An alternative to complete backyard freedom is a dog kennel or run which attaches to or surrounds the dog's house. This restricts some forms of movement, such as running, perhaps, but it does provide ample room for walking, climbing, jumping, and stretching. Another option is to fence off part of the yard and place the dog house in the enclosure. If you need to tether your dog to its house, make certain to use a fairly long lead so as not to hamper the animal's need to move and exercise his limbs.

A thick drape hung over the entrance to the dog's house will prevent drafts, thus keeping your dog warm and dry.

CLEANLINESS

No matter where your dog lives, either in or out of your home, be sure to keep him in surroundings that are as clean and sanitary as possible. His excrement should be removed and disposed of every day without fail. No dog should be forced to lie in his own feces. If your dog lives in his own house, the floor should be swept occasionally and the bedding should be changed regularly if it becomes soiled. Food and water dishes need to be scrubbed with hot water and detergent and rinsed well to remove all traces of soap. The water dish should be refilled with a supply of fresh water. The dog and his environment must be kept free of parasites (especially fleas and mosquitoes, which can carry disease) with products designed to keep these pests under control. Dog crates need frequent scrubbing, too, as do the floors of kennels and runs. Your pet must be kept clean and comfortable at all times; if you exercise strict sanitary control, you will keep disease and parasite infestation to a minimum.

Just as grooming and bathing keep your dog in a healthy condition, regular cleaning and disinfecting of his living area are important for his overall health. Many dogs that suffer from depression are subjected to

More and more cities and towns are requiring dog owners to clean up after their pets. Commercial pooper scoopers can make the clean-up easy and efficient. They are also helpful for backyard sanitation.

poorly maintained quarters. Your dog's physical and psychological well being are closely related. A clean dog is a healthy and happy dog.

EXERCISE

A well-balanced diet and regular medical attention from a qualified veterinarian are essential in promoting good health for your dog, but so is daily exercise to keep him fit and mentally alert. Dogs that have been confined all day while their owners are at work or school need special attention. There should be some time set aside make this daily ritual more pleasant both for themselves and their canine companions by combining the walk with a little "roughhousing," that is to say, a bit of fun and togetherness.

Whenever possible, take a stroll to an empty lot, a playground, or a nearby park. Attach a long lead to your dog's collar, and let him run and jump and tone his body through

Large outdoor pens are used by many breeding, boarding, and medical professionals. Always inspect the facility before leaving your dog in any professional's care.

each day for play—a romp with a family member, perhaps. Not everyone is lucky enough to let his dog run through an open meadow or along a sandy beach, but even a ten-minute walk in the fresh air will do. Dogs that are house-bound, particularly those that live in apartments, need to be walked out-of-doors after each meal so that they can relieve themselves. Owners can aerobic activity. This will help him burn calories and will keep him trim, and it will also help relieve tension and stress that may have had a chance to develop while you were away all day. For people who work Monday through Friday, weekend jaunts can be especially beneficial, since there will be more time to spend with your canine friend. You might

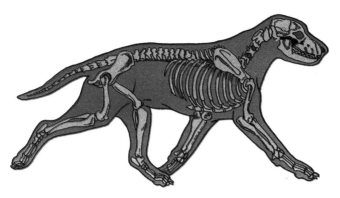

Responsible breeding practices, regular exercise, and proper nutrition all contribute to sound bone development.

want to engage him in a simple game of fetch with a stick or a rubber ball. Even such basic tricks as rolling over, standing on the hindlegs, or jumping up (all of which can be done inside the home as well) can provide additional exercise. But if you plan to challenge your dog with a real workout to raise his heart rate, remember not to push him too hard without first warming up with a brisk walk. Don't forget to "cool him down" afterwards with a rhythmic trot until his heart rate returns to normal. Some dog owners jog with their dogs or take them along on bicycle excursions.

At the very least, however, play with your dog every day to keep him in good shape physically and mentally. If you can walk him outdoors, or better yet run with him in a more vigorous activity, by all means do it. Don't neglect your pet and leave him confined

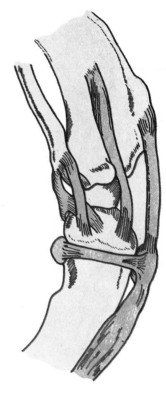

The knee joint is also known as the stifle joint. It is formed by the articulation of the upper and lower leg.

79

Accommodations

for long periods without attention from you or time for exercise.

EXERCISING FOR YOU AND YOUR DOG

Dogs are like people. They come in three weights: overweight, underweight, and the correct weight. It is fair to say that most dogs are in better shape than most humans who own them. The reason for this is that most dogs accept exercise without objection—people do not! Follow your dog's lead towards exercise and the complete enjoyment of the outdoors—your dog is the ideal work-out partner. There are toys at your local pet shop which are designed just for that purpose: to allow you to play and exercise with your dog. Here are a few recommended exercise toys for you and your dog.

Flying discs can make exercise exciting.

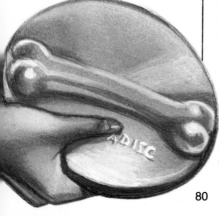

Frisbee® Flying Discs*

Who hasn't seen or heard of a Frisbee® flying disc? This flying-saucer–like toy is available in three or more sizes. The small size is 10 cm (4″); the medium size is about 15 cm (6″) and the larger size is 23 cm (9″). The size of the flying disc has little to do with the size of the dog—small puppies chase anything; some larger dogs chase nothing. The advantage of the larger disc is that it is the same size as the toy made for humans only! Start with the size that you think is best suited for your dog. What is much more important is the material from which the flying disc is made; *soft un-chew-worthy plastic flying discs are not good for dogs.*

Most people play with these polyethylene discs and use these same discs to play with their dogs. Polyethylene plastic discs usually last an hour or so. Every time the dog grabs it, his teeth dig into the cheap plastic, leaving an imprint. In a short while the disc is not useable— and even worse, it may be dangerous, since the dog can break off a chunk and swallow it, or the distorted disc can swerve out of control and hit someone.

*Frisbee® is a trademark of the Kransco Company, California, and is used for their brand of flying disc.

80

e sure that you do not throw the
ing disc where your dog can injure
mself. Open spaces where cars are
t permitted or a park are most ideal.

ylon Discs

Your pet shop will have a nylon
sc that has a dog bone molded
to the top of it. While this may
ok silly at first, the advantage is
mple. When a typical Frisbee®
nds on a flat surface, the dog
ay be unable to grasp it with its
outh or turn it over with its

paw. Thus frustrated, the dog
loses interest in the game and
you will have to fetch it yourself.
The nylon disc with the bone
molded into the top of it allows
the dog the option of flipping it
over with its paw or grasping it
with its mouth. It also has more
capacity; thus you can use it as a
food or water dish on these
outings. The nylon disc may also
be flavored and scented, besides
being annealed, so your dog can
find it more easily if it gets lost in
the woods or high grass.

ny owners complain that plastic flying discs are destroyed quickly by their dogs,
king an otherwise fun pastime an expensive outing. Flying discs made of an-
led nylon are proven to last longer and thereby provide hours of enjoyable, af-
able exercise for you and your dog.

Accommodations

Tug Toys

A tug toy is a hard rubber, cheap plastic, or polyurethane toy which allows a dog and his owner to have a game of tug-o-war. The owner grips one end while the dog grips the other—then they pull. The polyurethane flexible tug toy is the best on the market at the present time. Your pet shop will have one to show you. The polyurethane toys are clear in color and stay soft forever. Cheap plastic tug toys are indisputably dangerous, and the hard-rubber tug toys get brittle too fast and are too stiff for most dogs; however, there is a difference in price—just ask the advice of any shop operator.

Most every dog loves a challenging tug of war. Tug toys of sturdy polyurethane and strong cotton floss are favorites of many dogs.

Balls made of annealed nylon make fetching safe, pleasing and hygienic for your dog. Their virtually indestructible construction prevents the dog from tearing pieces of the ball and ingesting them, and the appealing scent inspires an enthusiastic retrieve. When worn, as shown here, nylon balls should be replaced with new ones.

Balls

Nobody has to tell you about playing ball with your dog. The reminder you may need is that you should not throw the ball where traffic might interfere with the dog's catching or fetching of it. The ball should not be cheap plastic (a dog's worst enemy as far as toys are concerned) but made of a substantial material. Balls made of nylon are practically indestructible, but they are very hard and must be rolled, never thrown. The same balls made of polyurethane are great—they bounce and are soft. The Nylabone® and Gumabone® balls are scented and flavored, and dogs can easily find them when lost.

Other manufacturers make balls of almost every substance, including plastic, cotton, and wood. Billiard balls, baseballs, tennis balls, and so on, have all been used by dog owners who want their dogs to play with them in a game of catch. A strong caveat is that you use only those balls made especially for dogs.

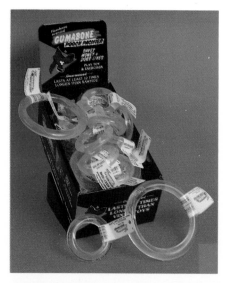

With the variety of safe, exercise-oriented chew products available, there is little excuse for a sedentary, plaque-infested existence to persist in an otherwise healthy dog.

Housebreaking and Training

Housebreaking can be the groundwork on which all future training is based. The two most commonly recommended methods involve paper training and crate training. When paper training is used, owners often employ litter boxes lined with paper to limit the area and make clean-up fast and easy.

HOUSEBREAKING

The new addition to your family may already have received some basic house training before his arrival in your home. If he has not, remember that a puppy will want to relieve himself about half a dozen times a day; it is up to you to specify where and when he should "do his business." Housebreaking is your first training concern and should begin the moment you bring the puppy home.

Ideally, puppies should be taken outdoors after meals, as a full stomach will exert pressure on the bladder and colon. What goes into the dog must eventually come out; the period after his meal is the most natural and appropriate time. When he eliminates, he should be praised, for this will increase the likelihood of the same thing happening after every meal. He should also be encouraged to use the same area and will probably be attracted to it after frequent use.

Some veterinarians maintain that a puppy can learn to urinate

Housebreaking and Training

and defecate on command, if properly trained. The advantage of this conditioning technique is that your pet will associate the act of elimination with a particular word of your choice rather than with a particular time or place which might not always be convenient or available. So whether you are visiting an unfamiliar place or don't want to go outside with your dog in sub-zero temperatures, he will still be able to relieve himself when he hears the specific command word. Elimination will occur after this "trigger" phrase or word sets up a conditioned reflex in the dog, who will eliminate anything contained in his bladder or bowel upon hearing it. The shorter the word, the more you can repeat it and imprint it on your dog's memory.

Your chosen command word should be given simultaneously with the sphincter opening events in order to achieve perfect and rapid conditioning. This is why it is important to familiarize yourself with the tell-tale signs preceding your puppy's elimination process. Then you will be prepared to say the word at the crucial moment. There is usually a sense of urgency on the dog's part; he may follow a sniffing and circling pattern which you will soon recognize. It is important to use the command in his usual area only when you know the puppy

can eliminate, i.e., when his stomach or bladder is full. He will soon learn to associate the act with the word. One word of advice, however, if you plan to try out this method: never use the puppy's name or any other word which he might frequently hear about the house—you can imagine the result!

Finally, remember that any training takes time. Such a conditioned response can be obtained with intensive practice with any normal, healthy dog over six weeks of age. Even Pavlov's salivating dogs required fifty repetitions before the desired response was achieved. Patience and persistence will eventually produce results—do not lose heart!

Indoors, sheets of newspapers can be used to cover the specific area where your dog should relieve himself. These should be placed some distance away from his sleeping and feeding area, as a puppy will not urinate or defecate where he eats. When the newspapers are changed, the bottom papers should be placed on top of the new ones in order to reinforce the purpose of the papers by scent as well as by sight. The puppy should be praised during or immediately after he has made use of this particular part of the room. Each positive reinforcement increases the possibility of his using that area again.

When he arrives, it is advisable to limit the puppy to one room, usually the kitchen, as it most likely has a linoleum or easily washable floor surface. Given the run of the house, the sheer size of the place will seem overwhelming and confusing and he might leave his "signature"

PATIENCE, PERSISTENCE, AND PRAISE

As with a human baby, you must be patient, tolerant, and understanding of your pet's mistakes, making him feel loved and wanted, not rejected and isolated. You wouldn't hit a baby for soiling his diapers, as you

An anchored lead can be the solution to a yard without a fence.

on your furniture or clothes! There will be time later to familiarize him gradually with his new surroundings.

would realize that he was not yet able to control his bowel movements; be as compassionate with your canine infant. Never rub his nose in his excreta. Never indulge in the common practice of punishing him with a rolled-up newspaper. Never hit a puppy with your hand. He will only become "hand-shy" and learn to fear you. Usually the punishment is meted out sometime after the offense and loses its efficacy, as the bewildered dog cannot connect the two events. Moreover, by association, he will soon learn to be afraid of you and anything to do with newspapers—including, perhaps, that area where he is *supposed* to relieve himself!

Most puppies are eager to please. Praise, encouragement, and reward (particularly the food variety) will produce far better results than any scolding or physical punishment. Moreover, it is far better to dissuade your puppy from doing certain things, such as chewing on chair legs or other furniture, by making those objects particularly distasteful to him. Some pet shops stock bitter apple sprays or citronella compounds for application to furniture legs. If these are ineffective, you could smear them with a generous amount of hot chili sauce or cayenne pepper mixed with petroleum jelly, for example. This would make it seem as if the object itself was administering the

From the moment you bring your dog home, the rules of the house must be enforced to ensure a consistently obedient home companion.

Professionals cite that housebreaking on newspapers can cause some dogs to believe that it is always okay to excrete on papers, regardless of location. Housebreaking pads are used by many cautious owners.

punishment whenever he attempted to chew it. He probably wouldn't need a second reminder!

Remember that the reason a dog has housebreaking or behavior problems is because his owner has allowed them to develop. This is why you must begin as you intend to continue, letting your dog know what is acceptable and unacceptable behavior. It is also important that you be consistent in your demands; you cannot feed him from the dining room table one day and then punish him when he begs for food from your dinner guests.

TRAINING

You will want the newest member of your family to be welcomed by everyone; this will not happen if he urinates in every room of the house or barks all night! He needs training in the correct forms of behavior in this new human world. You cannot expect your puppy to become the perfect pet overnight. He needs your help in his socialization process. Training greatly facilitates and enhances the relationship of the dog to his owner and to the rest of society. A successfully trained dog can be taken anywhere and behave well with anyone. Indeed, it is that one crucial word—*training*—which can transform an aggressive animal into a peaceful, well-behaved pet. Now, how does this "transformation" take place?

Some owners of small dogs use a figure-eight-style harness as a means of restraint.

Collars should always be worn, with identification tag and license attached.

WHEN AND HOW TO TRAIN

Like housebreaking, training should begin as soon as the puppy enters the house. The formal training sessions should be short but frequent, for example, ten to fifteen minute periods three times a day. These are much more effective than long, tiring sessions of half an hour which might soon become boring. You are building your relationship with your puppy during these times, so make them as enjoyable as possible. It is a good idea to have these sessions *before* the puppy's meal, not after it when he wouldn't feel like exerting himself; the dog will then associate something pleasurable with his training sessions and look forward to them.

E COLLAR AND LEASH

Your puppy should become ed to a collar and leash as on as possible. If he is very

e variety of canine collars and shes available surely allows for the rsonal touch.

young, a thin, choke-chain collar can be used, but you will need a larger and heavier one for training when he is a little older. Remember to have his name and address on an identification tag attached to his collar, as you don't want to lose your pet if he

A choke collar can be an effective training tool when used properly.

should happen to leave your premises and explore the neighborhood!

Let the puppy wear his collar until he is used to how it feels. After a short time he will soon become accustomed to it and you can attach the leash. He might resist your attempts to lead him or simply sit down and refuse to budge. Fight him for a few minutes, tugging on the leash if necessary, then let him relax for the day. He won't be trained until he learns that he must obey the pull under any circumstance, but this will take a few sessions. Remember that a dog's period of concentration is short, so LITTLE and OFTEN is the wisest course of action—and patience is the password to success.

GIVING COMMANDS

When you begin giving your puppy simple commands, make them as short as possible and use the same word with the same meaning at all times, for example, "Heel," "Sit," and "Stay." You must be consistent otherwise your puppy will become confused. The dog's name should prefix all commands to attract his attention. Do not become impatient with him however many times you have to repeat your command.

A good way to introduce the "Come" command is by calling the puppy when his meal is

ady. Once this is learned, you
n call your pet to you at will,
vays remembering to praise
n for his prompt obedience.
is "reward," or positive
nforcement, is such a crucial
rt of training that a Director of
e New York Academy of Dog
aining constructed his whole
aching program upon the
ethods of "Love, Praise, and
ward." Incidentally, if you use
e command "Come," use it
ery time. Don't switch to
ome here" or "Come boy," as
s will only confuse your dog.
It is worth underlining the fact
at punishment is an ineffective
aching technique. We have
eady seen this in
usebreaking. For example, if
ur pup should run away, it

A puppy's collar should be light and comfortable, yet still effectively secure the dog.

would be senseless to beat him
when he eventually returns; he
would only connect the
punishment with his return, not
with running away! In addition, it
is unwise to call him to you to
punish him, as he will soon learn
not to respond when you call his
name.

ead that allows for a sure, comfortable grip is a training necessity. Introduce your w dog to the lead slowly. When he becomes comfortable with it, training can gin.

Housebreaking and Training

SOME SPECIFIC COMMANDS

"Sit" This is one of the easiest and most useful commands for your dog to learn, so it is a good idea to begin with it. The only equipment required is a leash, a collar, and a few tasty tidbits. Take your dog out for some exercise before his meal. After about five minutes, call him to you, praise him when he arrives,

A popular item with owners who love to walk their dogs is the harness. The harness fits comfortably around the dog's forequarters and displaces the pressure of the owner's tug on the lead.

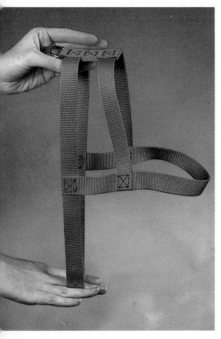

and slip his collar on him. Hold the leash tightly in your right hand; this should force the dog head up and focus his attention on you. As you say "Sit" in a loud, clear voice, with your left hand press steadily on his rump until he is in a sitting position. soon as he is in the correct position, praise him and give him the tidbit you have in your hand Now wait a few minutes to let him rest and repeat the routine Through repetition, the dog soon associates the word with the act Never make the lesson too long Eventually your praise will be reward enough for your puppy Other methods to teach this command exist, but this one, executed with care and moderation, has proven the most effective.

"Sit-Stay/Stay" To teach your pet to remain in one place or "stay" on your command, first all order him to the sitting position at your side. Lower your left hand with the flat of your palm in front of his nose and your fingers pointing downwards. Hold the leash high and taut behind his head so that he cannot move. Speak the command "Sit-stay" and, as you are giving it, step in front of him Repeat the command and tighten the leash so the animal cannot follow you. Walk completely around him, repeating the command and keeping him motionless by holding the leash at arm's length above him to check his movement. When he remains in this position for about fifteen seconds, you can begin the second part of the training. You will have to exchange the leash for a nylon cord or rope about twenty to thirty feet long. Repeat the whole routine from the beginning and be ready to prevent any movement towards you with a sharp "Sit-stay." Move around him in ever-widening circles until you are about fifteen feet away from him. If he still remains seated, you can pat yourself on the back! One useful thing to remember is that the dog makes associations with what you say, how you say it, and what you do while you are saying it. Give this command in a firm, clear tone of voice, perhaps using an admonishing forefinger raised, warning the dog to "stay."

Two training accessories especially common with obedience trial enthusiasts are the hurdle (above) and the dumbbell (below). To see dogs performing with these and other field accessories, attend an obedience competition. Remember that training requires consistency and commitment, but the rewards are well worth the effort.

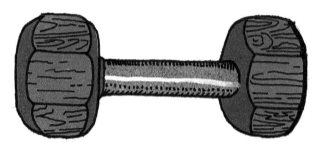

Housebreaking and Training

"Heel" When you walk your dog, you should hold the leash firmly in your right hand. The dog should walk on your left so you have the leash crossing your body. This enables you to have greater control over the dog.

Let your dog lead you for the first few moments so that he fully understands that freedom can be his if he goes about it properly. He already knows that when he wants to go outdoors the leash and collar are necessary, so he has respect for the leash. Now, if he starts to pull in one direction while walking, all you do is *stop walking.* He will walk a few steps and then find that he can't walk any further. He will then turn and look into your face. *This is the crucial point!* Just stand there for a moment and stare right back at him . . . now walk another ten feet and stop again. Again your dog will probably walk to the end of the leash, find he can't go any further, and turn around and look again. If he starts to pull and jerk, just stand there. After he quiets down, bend down and comfort him, as he may be frightened. Keep up this training until he learns not to outwalk you.

Once the puppy obeys the pull of the leash, half of your training is accomplished. "Heeling" is a necessity for a well-behaved dog, so teach him to walk beside you, head even with your knee.

Nothing looks sadder than a big dog taking his helpless owner for a walk. It is annoying to passers-by and other dog owners to have a large dog, however friendly, bear down on them and entangle dogs, people, and packages.

To teach your dog, start off walking briskly, saying "Heel" in a firm voice. Pull back with a sharp jerk if he lunges ahead, and if he lags repeat the command and tug on the leash, not allowing him to drag behind. After the dog has learned to heel at various speeds on leash, you

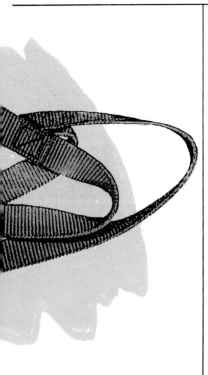

ready or when you wish to play with him or praise him. Outdoors such a response is more difficult to achieve, if he is happily playing by himself or with other dogs, so he must be trained to come to you when he is called. To teach him to come, let him reach the end of a long lead, then give the command, gently pulling him towards you at the same time. As soon as he associates the word *come* with the action of moving towards you, pull only when he does not respond immediately. As he starts to come, move back to make him learn that he must come from a distance as well as when he is close to you. Soon you may be able to practice without a leash, but if he is slow to come or actively disobedient, go to him and pull him toward you, repeating the command. Always remember to reward his successful completion of a task.

The lead is an essential tool for teaching such commands as "heel," "come," and "down."

can remove it and practice heeling free, but have it ready to snap on again as soon as he wanders.

"Come" Your dog has already learned to come to you when you call his name. Why? Because you only call him when his food is

"Down" Teaching the "down" command ideally begins while your dog is still a pup. During puppyhood your dog frequently will lie down, as this position is one of the dog's most natural positions. Invest some time, and keep close watch over your pup. Each time he begins to lie, repeat in a low convincing tone the word "down." If for the first day of training, you concur a majority of the dog's sitting with your commands and continue with reinforcement and moderate praise your pup should conquer the "down" command in no time.

Teaching the "down" command to a mature dog likely will require more effort. Although the lying position is still natural to a dog, his being forced into it is not. Some dogs may react with fear, anger, or confusion. Others may accept the process and prove quick learners. Have your

For the dog that responds with anger or aggression, attach a lead (and a muzzle) and have the dog sit facing you at a close distance. There should be a J-loop formed by the lead. With moderate force, relative to the size and strength of your dog, step on the J-loop, forcing the dog down, while repeating the command "down" in a low forceful tone. When the dog is down, moderate praise should

Threats and physical punishment have no place in the canine training process. The keys to effective training are patience, persistence, and praise.

dog sit and face you. If he is responsive and congenial, gently take his paws, and slowly pull them towards you; give the "down" command as he approaches the proper position. Repeat several times: moderate reinforcement of this procedure should prove rewardingly successful.

be given. If the dog proves responsive, you may attempt extending his legs to the "down" position—leaving the muzzle on, of course. Daily reinforcement of the training method will soon yield the desired results. The keys to remember are: patience, persistence, and praise.

ehavior Modification

Problems with the Barking og" and "Aggressive Behavior nd Dominance" are extracts om the veterinary monograph *anine Behavior* (a compilation f columns from *Canine ractice,* a journal published by eterinary Practice Publishing ompany).

ROBLEMS WITH THE ARKING DOG

One of the most frequent omplaints about canine ehavior is barking. Aside from 1e biting dog, the barking dog is robably the pet peeve of many on-dog owners. I know of at east one city in which owners of ogs that bark excessively, and or which there are complaints n file, are required to take steps o eliminate the barking.

Canine practitioners are rawn into problems with arking when they are asked for 1eir advice in helping an owner ome up with a solution or, as a 1st resort, when they are equested to perform a ebarking operation or even uthanasia. In this column I will eal with some of the factors 1at apparently cause dogs to ark and suggest some orrective approaches.

Barking is, of course, a natural esponse for many dogs. They ave an inherited predisposition o bark as an alarm when other ogs or people approach their erritory. Alarm barking makes

A problem facing many dog owners is excessive vocalization. Fortunately, a number of correctives have proven successful.

many dogs valuable as household watchdogs and is not necessarily undesirable behavior. With a different vocal tone and pattern, dogs bark when they are playing with each other. On occasion dogs have a tendency to bark back at other dogs or join in with other barking dogs.

In addition to inherited barking tendencies, dogs can also learn to bark if the barking is followed, at least sometimes, by a reward. Thus dogs may bark when they wish to come in the house or to get out of a kennel. Some dogs are trained to bark upon hearing the command "speak" for a food reward.

One of the first approaches to

Behavior Modification

take when discussing a barking problem is to determine if the behavior is a manifestation of a natural (inherited) tendency or is learned behavior which has been rewarded in the past.

Can Barking Be Extinguished?
Extinction, as a way of eliminating a behavioral problem, may be considered when it is clear that the behavior has been learned and when one can identify the specific rewarding or reinforcing factors that maintain the behavior.

For example, the dog that barks upon hearing the command "speak" is periodically rewarded with food and praise. If a dog is never, ever given food or praise again when it barks after being told to "speak," it will eventually stop this type of barking. This is the process of extinction and it implies that the

Reward in the form of treats is often effective.

behavior must be repeated but never again rewarded.

A more practical example of the possible use of extinction would be in dealing with the dog that apparently barks because, at least occasionally, it is allowed in the house. By not allowing the dog in the house until the barking has become very frequent and loud, the owners may have shaped the barking behavior to that which is the most objectionable. If the dog is never allowed in the house again when barking, the barking should eventually be extinguished—at least theoretically.

How Should Punishment Be Used? Sometimes it is not feasible to attempt to extinguish barking even if it seems to be the case that the behavior was learned. This brings up the advisability of punishment. Clients who seek advice in dealing with a barking problem may already have employed some type of punishment such as shouting at the dog or throwing something at it. That this type of punishment is ineffective is attested to by the fact that the client is seeking advice. By shouting at a dog or hitting, a person interferes with what effect the punishment may have on the behavior itself through the arousal of autonomic reactions and escape attempts or submissive responses by the dog.

The Water Bucket Approach

I am rather impressed by the ingenuity of some dog owners in coming up with ways to punish a dog for barking without being directly involved in administering the punishment. One such harried dog owner I talked to, who was also a veterinarian, was plagued by his dog's barking in the kennel commencing at about 2:30 a.m. every night. A platform to hold a bucket of water was constructed over the area of the kennel in which the dog usually chose to bark. Through a system of hinges, ropes, and pulleys, a mechanism was devised so that the dog owner could pull a rope from his bedroom window, dumping a bucket of water on the dog when he started to bark. The bucket was suspended such that once it was dumped, it uprighted itself and the owner could fill it again remotely by turning on a garden hose. After two appropriate dunkings, the dog's barking behavior was apparently eliminated.

With a little ingenuity, a bucket attached to a trap door can be constructed. Soaking the dog in this surprising manner can possibly extinguish a bad barking habit. Always take into consideration the weather conditions, the health and age of your dog, and the cause of the barking problem before embarking on the water-bucket cure.

In advising a client on the type of punishment discussed above, keep in mind one important consideration. From the time the owner is ready to administer punishment for barking, every attempt should be made to punish all undesirable barking from that point on and not to allow excessively long periods of barking to go unpunished. Thus it may be necessary to keep a dog indoors when away unless the dog will be punished for barking when the owner is gone.

Behavior Modification

Alternative Responses Barking dogs are, and probably always will be, one of the enduring problems of dog owners. Barking is relatively effortless, and it is such a natural response for many dogs that it is admittedly hard to eliminate with either punishment or a program of conditioning non-barking. In some instances it may be advisable to forget about eliminating barking and to suggest that the problem be dealt with by changing the circumstances which lead to barking. For example, a dog that barks continuously in the backyard while the owners are away may not bark if left in the house while they are gone. But the problem of keeping the dog in the house may be related to inadequate house training or the dog's shedding hair or climbing onto the furniture. It may be easier to correct these latter behavioral problems than it is to change the barking behavior.

Especially for aggressive dogs, muzzles can prevent both injuries and lawsuits.

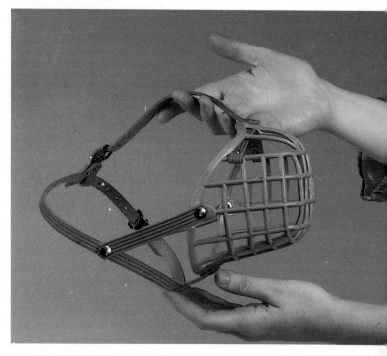

104

AGGRESSIVE BEHAVIOR AND DOMINANCE

Aggressiveness can have many causes. Determining what kind of aggression an animal is manifesting is a prerequisite to successful treatment of the behavior. A frequent problem that is presented to the practitioner is one of aggression related to dominance.

Dogs, which are social animals, have a hierarchal system of dominance within their pack. This predisposition to take a dominant or submissive position relative to fellow canines also occurs in relationship to people. Only in unusual situations would a submissive dog threaten a dominant animal, and almost never would it physically assault its superior. The dominant dog, however, frequently threatens submissive individuals to maintain its position. In a household setting, a person may be the object of threats, and when the person backs off, the dog's position is reassured. The aggressive behavior is also reinforced, and when behavior is reinforced it is likely to recur.

Case History The following is a typical case history of a dog presented for aggression stemming from dominance.

Max was a two-year-old intact male Cocker Spaniel. He had been acquired by Mr. Smith, one year prior to his owner's marriage, as a puppy. He liked and was well liked by both Mr. and Mrs. Smith. He frequently solicited and received attention from both people. However, several times over the last few months, Max had snapped at Mrs. Smith and repeatedly growled at her. A detailed anamnesis revealed that such incidents usually occurred in situations where the dog wanted his own way or did not want to be bothered. He would growl if asked to move off a chair or if persistently commanded to do a specific task. He growled if Mrs. Smith came between him and a young female Cocker Spaniel acquired a year ago. He also refused to let Mrs. Smith take anything from his possession.

Behavior Modification

Max never showed any of these aggressive behaviors toward Mr. Smith or strangers. Admittedly he did not have much opportunity to demonstrate such behaviors toward strangers. A description of the dog's body and facial postures and circumstances under which the

Dogs can become possessive of their playthings or aggressive in defense of their territory.

aggression occurred did not indicate that this was a case of fear-induced aggression, but rather one of assertion of dominance.

Mrs. Smith's reaction to the aggression was always to retreat, and, hence, the dog was rewarded for his assertiveness. She had never physically disciplined the dog and was afraid to do so. To encourage her to physically take control of the dog would likely have resulted in her being bitten. The dominance-submissive relationship had to be reversed in a more subtle manner.

Instructions to Client Mrs. Smith was instructed to avoid all situations which might evoke any aggressive signs from Max. This was to prevent any further reinforcement of his growling and threats.

Both she and her husband were not to indiscriminately pet or show affection towards the dog. For the time being, if Max solicited attention from Mr. Smith, he was to ignore the dog. Mrs. Smith was to take advantage of Max's desire for attention by giving him a command which he had to obey before she praised and petted him. She was also to take advantage of high motivation levels for other activities whenever such situations arose. Max had to obey a command before she gave him anything—

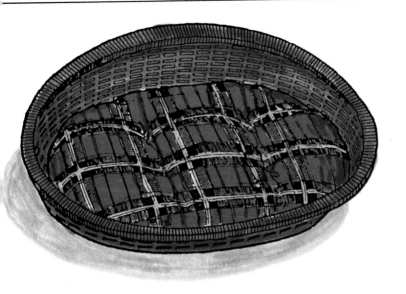

efore she petted him, before
he let him out or in, etc.

Mrs. Smith also was to
ssume total care of the dog and
ecome "the source of all good
hings in life" for Max. She was
o feed him, take him on walks,
lay with him, etc.

Mrs. Smith also spent 5–10
minutes a day teaching Max
imple parlor tricks and
bedience responses for
oveted food rewards as well as
raise. These were entirely fun
nd play sessions—but within a
ew days the dog had acquired
he habit of quickly responding
o commands. And this habit
ransferred over to the non-game
ituations.

Results Within a few weeks,

*The dog's bed can become an object
of possession. The dog can come to
perceive it as his territory, not allowing
others to come near. In such instances
behavior modification may be
necessary.*

Max had ceased to growl and
threaten Mrs. Smith in situations
that he previously had. He would
move out of her way or lie quietly
when she would pass by him.
She could order him off the
furniture and handle the female
Cocker Spaniel without eliciting
threats from Max.

Mrs. Smith still felt that she
would not be able to take the
objects from Max's possession.
Additional instructions were

Behavior Modification

A dog comes to associate the pleasure of receiving a treat with the action immediately preceding it. Treats are effective in shaping behavior and building a relationship with your pet when they are used judiciously and in moderation.

given to her. She then began placing a series of objects at progressively closer distances to the dog while the dog was in a sit-stay position. After she placed the object on the floor for a short time, she would pick it up. If the dog was still in a sit-stay (which it always was), he received a reward of cheese and verbal praise. Eventually the objects were to be placed and

removed from directly in front of the dog. At first she was to use objects that the dog did not care much about and then progressively use more coveted items. This was what she was supposed to do, but before she actually had completed the program she called in excitedly to report that she had taken a piece of stolen food and a household ornament from Max's mouth. And he didn't even object! She said she had calmly told Max to sit. He did. He was so used to doing so, in the game and other situations, that the response was now automatic. She walked over, removed the item from his mouth, and praised him.

Mrs. Smith did resume the systematic presentation of objects and put the dog on an intermittent schedule of food and praise reinforcement during the practice sessions. Mr. Smith again began interacting with Max.

A progress check six months later indicated Max was still an obedient dog and had definitely assumed a submissive position relative to both of his owners. The dominance hierarchy between Max and Mrs. Smith had been reversed *without resorting to any physical punishment.* Mrs. Smith was instructed to reinforce her dominance position by frequently giving Max a command and reinforcing him for the appropriate response.

Summary The essential elements in treatment of such cases are as follows. First, of course, there must be a correct diagnosis of what kind of aggressive behavior is occurring. During the course of treatment, the submissive person(s) should avoid all situations that might evoke an aggressive attitude by the dog. All other family members should totally ignore the dog during the treatment interim. The person most dominated by the dog should take over complete care of the dog in addition to spending 5–10 minutes a day teaching the dog tricks or simple obedience commands (sit-stay is a useful one to gain control of the dog in subsequent circumstances). These should be fun-and-games situations. Food rewards are highly recommended in addition to simple praise.

The person submissive to the dog should take the opportunity to give the dog a command, which must be obeyed, before doing anything pleasant for the dog.

It must be emphasized to the owner that no guarantee can be made that the dog will never threaten or be aggressive again. What is being done, as with all other aggression cases, is an attempt to reduce the likelihood, incidence, and intensity of occurrence of the aggressive behavior.

DESTRUCTIVE TENDENCIES

It is ironical but true that a dog's destructive behavior in the home may be proof of his love for his owner. He may be trying to get more attention from his owner or, in other cases, may be expressing his frustration at his owner's absence. An abundance

Some crates have wire-mesh fronts while others do not. The primary consideration in choosing a crate is its ventilation.

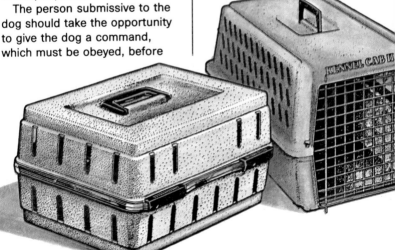

Behavior Modification

of unused energy may also contribute to a dog's destructive behavior, and therefore the owner should ensure that his dog has, at least, twenty minutes of vigorous exercise a day.

As a dog's destructive tendencies may stem from his desire to get more attention from his owner, the latter should devote specific periods each day to his dog when he is actively interacting with him. Such a period should contain practice obedience techniques during which the owner can reward the dog with his favorite food as well as praise and affection.

Planned departure conditioning is one specific technique which has been used to solve the problem of destructive tendencies in a puppy. It eventually ensures the dog's good behavior during the owner's absence. A series of

Not just great recreational devices to channel doggie tensions, the Gumabone® products have been scientifically proven to reduce tartar and plaque build-up. These products are available in many shapes and sizes. Gumabone® products should be replaced regularly when they become excessively worn.

short departures, which are identical to real departures, should condition the dog to behave well in the owner's absence. How is this to be achieved? Initially, the departures are so short (2–5 minutes) that the dog has no opportunity to be destructive. The dog is always rewarded for having been good when the owner returns. Gradually the duration of the departures is increased. The departure time is also varied so that the dog does not know when the owner is going to return. Since a different kind of behavior is now expected, it is best if a new stimulus or "atmosphere" is introduced into the training sessions to permit the dog to distinguish these departures as different from previous departures when he was destructive.

This new stimulus could be the sound of the radio or television. The association which the dog will develop is that whenever the "signal" or "stimulus" is on, the owner will return in an unknown

A proven safe chew product.

A safe tug toy.

period of time and, if the dog has not been destructive, he will be rewarded. As with the daily owner-dog interaction, the food reward is especially useful.

If the dog misbehaves during his owner's absence, the owner should speak sternly to him and isolate him from social contact for at least thirty minutes. (Puppies hate to be ignored.) Then the owner should conduct another departure of a shorter time and generously reward good behavior when he returns. The owner should progress slowly enough in the program so that once the departure has been initiated, the dog is never given an opportunity to make a mistake.

If planned departures are working satisfactorily, the departure time may gradually be extended to several hours. To reduce the dog's anxiety when left alone, he should be given a "safety valve" such as the indestructible Nylabone® to play with and chew on.

111

Health Care

From the moment you purchase your puppy, the most important person in both your lives becomes your veterinarian. His professional advice and treatment will ensure the good health of your pet. The vet is the first person to call when illness or accidents occur. Do *not* try to be your own veterinarian or apply human remedies to canine diseases. However, just as you would keep a first aid kit handy for minor injuries sustained by members of your family at home, so you should keep a similar kit prepared for your pet.

First aid for your dog would consist of stopping any bleeding, cleaning the wound, and

Even in your own back yard, injuries can occur.

preventing infection. Thus your kit might contain medicated powder, gauze bandages, and adhesive tape to be used in case of cuts. If the cut is deep and bleeding profusely, the bandage should be applied very tightly to help in the formation of a clot. A tight bandage should not be kept in place longer than necessary, so take your pet to the veterinarian immediately.

Walking or running on a cut pad prevents the cut from healing. Proper suturing of the cut and regular changing of the bandages should have your pet's wound healed in a week to ten days. A minor cut should be covered with a light bandage, for you want as much air as possible to reach the wound. Do not apply wads of cotton to a wound; they will stick to the area and may cause contamination.

You should also keep some hydrogen peroxide available, as it is useful in cleaning wounds and is also one of the best and simplest emetics known. Cotton applicator swabs are useful for applying ointment or removing debris from the eyes. A pair of tweezers should also be kept handy for removing foreign bodies from the dog's neck, head or body.

Nearly everything a dog might contract in the way of sickness has basically the same set of symptoms: loss of appetite, diarrhea, dull eyes, dull coat,

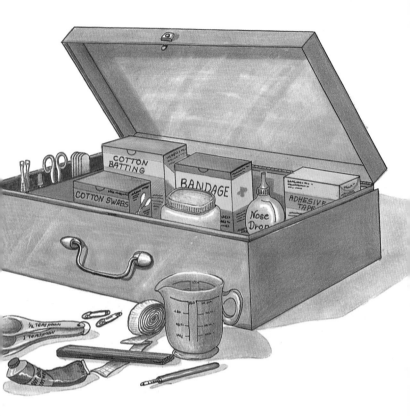

hen emergencies occur, it pays to be prepared. A first-aid kit, well stocked with ommon sense medical accessories and tools, is helpful to have available at all mes.

arm and/or runny nose, and a igh temperature. Therefore, it is ost important to take his mperature at the first sign of ness. To do this, you will need rectal thermometer which ould be lubricated with etroleum jelly. Carefully insert it to the rectum, holding it in ace for at least two minutes. It ust be held firmly; otherwise

there is the danger of its being sucked up into the rectum or slipping out, thus giving an inaccurate reading. The normal temperature for a dog is between 101° and 102.5°F. If your pet is seriously ill or injured in an accident, your veterinarian will advise you what to do before he arrives.

SWALLOWING FOREIGN OBJECTS

Most of us have had experience with a child swallowing a foreign object. Usually it is a small coin; occasionally it may be a fruit pit or something more dangerous. Dogs, *as a general rule,* will not swallow anything which isn't edible. There are, however, many dogs that swallow pebbles or small shiny objects such as pins, coins, and bits of cloth and plastic. This is especially true of dogs that are offered so-called "chew toys."

Chew toys are available in many sizes, shapes, colors and materials. Some even have whistles which sound when the dog's owner plays with it or when the dog chomps on it quickly. Most dogs attack the whistle first, doing everything possible to make it stop squeaking. Obviously, if the whistle is made of metal, a dog can injure its mouth, teeth, or tongue. Therefore, *never* buy a "squeak toy" made with a metal whistle.

Other chew toys are made of vinyl, a cheap plastic which is soft to the touch and pliable. Most of the cute little toys that are figures of animals or people are made of this cheap plastic. They are sometimes hand-painted in countries where the cost of such labor is low. Not only is the paint used dangerous

to dogs, because of the lead content, but the vinyl tears easily and is usually destroyed by the dog during the first hour. Small bits of vinyl may be ingested and cause blockage of the intestine. You are, therefore, reminded of these things before you buy anything vinyl for your dog!

Very inexpensive dog toys, usually found in supermarkets and other low-price venues, may be made of polyethylene. These are to be avoided completely, as this cheap plastic is, for some odd reason, attractive to dogs. Dogs destroy the toy in minutes and sometimes swallow the indigestible bits and pieces that come off. Most pet shops carry only safe toys.

WHAT TOYS ARE SAFE FOR DOGS?

Hard Rubber Toys made of hard rubber are usually safe for dogs, providing the toy is made of 100% hard rubber and not a compound of rubber and other materials. The rubber must be "virgin" and not re-ground from old tires, tubes, and other scrap rubber products. The main problem with rubber, even 100% virgin rubber, is that it oxidizes quickly, especially when subjected to the ultraviolet rays of the sun and a dog's saliva. The rubber then tends to be brittle, to crack, to dust off, and to be extremely dangerous to dogs that like swallowing things.

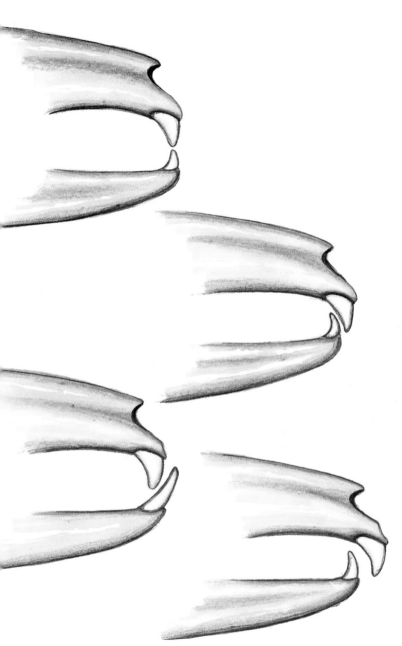

From top to bottom, *the four common bite types are: (a) level, (b) scissors, (c) un-*
dershot, and (d) overshot. Different breeds have different bite types and one bite
type may be desirable in your breed and most undesirable in another.

Health Care

Nylon Toys Toys made of nylon could well be the safest of all toys, *providing the nylon is annealed.* Nylon that is not annealed is very fragile ,and if you smash it against a hard surface, it might shatter like glass. The same is true when the weather is cold and the nylon drops below freezing. Thus far there is only one line of dog toys that is made of annealed virgin nylon—Nylabone®. These toys are not only annealed but they are flavored and scented. The flavors and scents, such as hambone, are undetectable by humans, but dogs seem to find them attractive.

Some nylon bones have the flavor sprayed on them or molded into them. These cheaper bones are easy to detect—just smell them. If you discern an odor, you know they are poorly made. The main

The inherent need to chew is strong in dogs of all ages. The canine's constant chewing of his favorite chew products will necessitate their regular replacement. When bone becomes frayed, it's time to replace it.

problem with the nylon toys that have an odor is that they are not annealed and they "smell up" the house or car. The dog's saliva dilutes the odor of the bone, and when he drops it on your rug, this odor attaches itself to the rug and is quite difficult to remove.

Annealed nylon may be the best there is ,but it is not 100% safe. The Nylabone® dog chews are really meant to be Pooch Pacifiers®. This trade name indicates the effect intended for the dog, which is to relieve the tension in your excited puppy or adult dog who is left alone or wants to "spite" you. Instead of chewing up the furniture or some other object, he chews up his Nylabone® instead. Many dogs ignore the Nylabone® for weeks, suddenly attacking it when they have to relieve their doggie tensions.

Some dogs may have jaws strong enough to chomp off a piece of Nylabone®, but this is extremely rare. *One word of caution:* the Nylabone® should be replaced when the dog has chewed down the knuckle. Most dogs slowly scrape off small slivers of nylon which pass harmlessly through their digestive tract. The resultant frizzled bone actually becomes a toothbrush.

One of the great characteristics of nylon bones is that they can be boiled and

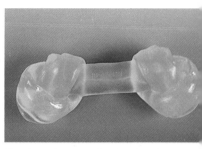

The Gumaknot® is the favorite chew item of many dogs.

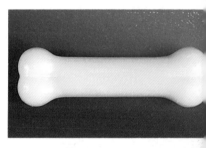

Above: The Nylabone® is an effective, proven-safe therapeutic device. **Below**: The Gumaball® is useful for outside recreation, exercise, and tooth care.

Doggie treats come in a wide variety of sizes, shapes, and flavors. While they can be useful as rewards and occasional tidbits, they do not satisfy the dog's need to chew. Treats are best used for what they are intended—as treats.

sterilized. If a dog loses interest in his Nylabone®, or it is too hard for him to chew due to his age and the condition of his teeth, you can cook it in some chicken or beef broth, allowing it to boil for 30 minutes. Let it cool down normally. It will then be perfectly sterile and re-flavored for the next dog. *Don't try this with plastic bones, as they will melt and ruin your pot.*

Polyurethane Toys Toys made of polyurethane are almost as good as nylon bones—but not quite. There are several brands on the market: ignore the ones which have scents that you can discern. Some of the scented polyurethane bones have an unbearable odor after the scent has rubbed off the bone and onto your rug or car seat. Again, look for the better-quality polyurethane toy. Gumabone® is

a flexible material, the same as used for making artificial hearts and the bumpers on automobiles, thus it is strong and stable. It is not as strong as Nylabone®, but many dogs like it because it is soft.

The most popular of the Gumabone® products made in polyurethane are the tug toys, balls, and Frisbee® flying discs. These items are almost clear in color, have the decided advantage of lasting a long time, and are useful in providing exercise for both a dog and his master or mistress.

Whatever dog toy you buy, be sure it is high quality. Pet shops, as a rule, carry the better-quality toys, while supermarkets seem to be concerned only with price. Of course there may be exceptions, but you are best advised to ask your local pet shop operator—or even your veterinarian—what toys are suitable for *your* dog.

In conclusion, if your dog is a swallower of foreign objects, don't give him anything cheap to chew on. If he swallows a coin, you can hardly blame the Treasury! Unless your dog is carefully supervised, use only the largest size Nylabone®, and replace it as soon as the dog chews down the knuckles. *Do not let the dog take the Nylabone® outdoors.* First of all he can hide and bury it, digging it up when his tensions rise. Then, too, all nylon becomes more brittle when it freezes, even Nylabone®.

IF YOUR PET SWALLOWS POISON

A poisoned dog must be treated instantly; any delay could cause his death. Different poisons act in different ways and require different treatments. If you know the dog has swallowed an acid, alkali, gasoline, or kerosene, do not induce vomiting. Give milk to dilute the poison and rush him to the vet. If you can find the bottle or container of poison, check the label to see if there is a recommended antidote. If not, try to induce vomiting by giving him a mixture of hydrogen peroxide and water. Mix the regular drugstore strength of hydrogen peroxide (3%) with an equal part of water, but do not attempt to pour it down your dog's throat, as that could cause inhalation pneumonia. Instead, simply pull the dog's lips away from the side of his mouth, making a pocket for depositing the liquid. Use at least a tablespoonful of the mixture for every ten pounds of your dog's

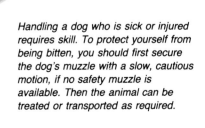

Handling a dog who is sick or injured requires skill. To protect yourself from being bitten, you should first secure the dog's muzzle with a slow, cautious motion, if no safety muzzle is available. Then the animal can be treated or transported as required.

119

weight. He will vomit in about two minutes. When his stomach has settled, give him a teaspoonful of Epsom salts in a little water to empty the intestine quickly. The hydrogen peroxide, on ingestion, becomes oxygen and water and is harmless to your dog; it is the best antidote for phosphorus, which is often used in rat poisons. After you have administered this emergency treatment to your pet and his stomach and bowels have been emptied, rush him to your veterinarian for further care.

DANGER IN THE HOME

There are numerous household products that can prove fatal if ingested by your pet. These include rat poison, antifreeze, boric acid, hand soap, detergents, insecticides, mothballs, household cleansers,

Water hemlock is one of the many poisonous plants that can cause serious complications if ingested by a canine.

bleaches, de-icers, polishes and disinfectants, paint and varnish removers, acetone, turpentine, and even health and beauty aids if ingested in large enough quantities. A word to the wise should be sufficient: what you would keep locked away from your two-year-old child should also be kept hidden from your pet.

There is another danger lurking within the home among the household plants, which are almost all poisonous, even if swallowed in small quantities. There are hundreds of poisonous plants around us, among which are: ivy leaves, cyclamen, lily of the valley, rhododendrons, tulip bulbs, azalea, wisteria, poinsettia

Suburban backyards are often fertile grounds for a variety of flowering plant types. Many of these pretty-to-the-eye plants can be harmful to a canine. Lily-of-the-valley is attractive and popular in some climates; it is, however, poisonous if ingested and should not be cultivated near the dog's living area.

Lactrodectus mactans, *better known as the black widow spider, is said to possess venom over 15 times as toxic as many rattlesnakes'. This spider most commonly occurs in warm climates. Owners are encouraged to inspect the dog's living area periodically for such lethal inhabitants.*

leaves, mistletoe, daffodils, delphiniums, foxglove leaves, the jimson weed—we cannot name them all. Rhubarb leaves, for example, either raw or cooked, can cause death or violent convulsions. Peach, elderberry, and cherry trees can cause cyanide poisoning if their bark is consumed.

There are also many insects that can be poisonous to dogs such as spiders, bees, wasps, and some flies. A few toads and frogs exude a fluid that can make a dog foam at the mouth—and even kill him—if he bites too hard!

There have been cases of dogs suffering nicotine poisoning by consuming the contents of full ashtrays which thoughtless smokers have left on the coffee table. Also, do not leave nails, staples, pins, or other sharp objects lying around. Likewise, don't let your puppy play with plastic bags which could suffocate him. Unplug, remove, or cover any electrical cords or wires near your dog. Chewing live wires could lead to severe mouth burns or death. Remember that an ounce of prevention is worth a pound of cure: keep all potentially dangerous objects out of your pet's reach.

Bufo marinus, *the giant toad, is a very large species of toad that, when provoked, will produce a secretion that is toxic if ingested. The giant toad can potentially be a canine killer.*

VEHICLE TRAVEL SAFETY

A dog should never be left alone in a car. It takes only a few minutes for the heat to become unbearable in the summer, and to drop to freezing in the winter.

A dog traveling in a car or truck should be well behaved. An undisciplined dog can be deadly in a moving vehicle. The dog should be trained to lie on the back seat of the vehicle. Allowing your dog to stick its head out of the window is unwise. The dog may jump or it may get something in its eye. Some manufacturers sell seat belts and car seats designed for dogs.

Traveling with your dog in the back of your pick-up truck is an unacceptable notion and dangerous to all involved.

PROTECT YOURSELF FIRST

In almost all first aid situations, the dog is in pain. He may indeed be in shock and not appear to be suffering, until you move him. Then he may bite your hand or resist being helped at all. So if you want to help your dog, help yourself first by tying his mouth closed. To do this, use a piece of strong cloth four inches wide and three feet long, depending on the size of the dog. Make a loop in the middle of the strip and slip it over his nose with the knot under his chin and over the bony part of his nose.

Pull it tight and bring the ends back around his head behind the ears and tie it tightly, ending with a bow knot for quick, easy release. Now you can handle the dog safely. As a dog perspires through his tongue, do not leave the "emergency muzzle" on any longer than necessary.

ADMINISTERING MEDICINE

When you are giving liquid medicine to your dog, it is a good idea to pull the lips away from the side of the mouth, form a lip pocket, and let the liquid trickle past the tongue. Remain at his side, never in front of the dog, as he may cough and spray you with the liquid. Moreover, you must never pour liquid medicine while the victim's tongue is drawn out, as inhalation pneumonia could be the disastrous result.

Medicine in pill form is best administered by forcing the dog's mouth open, holding his head back, and placing the capsule as far back on his tongue as you can reach. To do this: put the palm of your hand over the dog's muzzle (his foreface) with your fingers on one side of his jaw, your thumb

An injured dog can bite, rather unintentionally. A make-shift muzzle can be used in the case of an emergency. A tie or a torn piece of cloth can suffice.

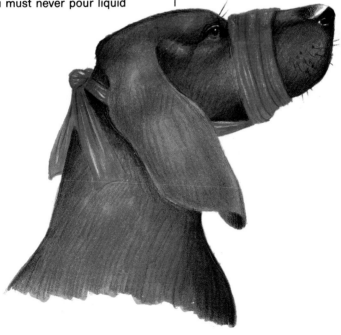

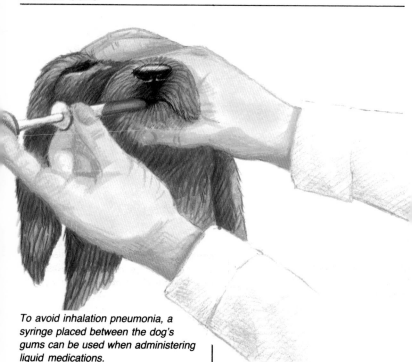

To avoid inhalation pneumonia, a syringe placed between the dog's gums can be used when administering liquid medications.

on the other. Press his lips hard against his teeth while using your other hand to pull down his lower jaw. With your two fingers, try to put the pill as far back on the dog's tongue as you can reach. Keep his mouth and nostrils closed and he should be forced to swallow the medicine. As the dog will not be feeling well, stroke his neck to comfort him and to help him swallow his medicine more easily. Do keep an eye on him for a few moments afterward, however, to make certain that he does not spit it out.

IN CASE OF AN ACCIDENT

It is often difficult for you to assess the dog's injuries after a road accident. He may appear normal, but there might be internal hemorrhaging. A vital organ could be damaged or ribs broken. Keep the dog as quiet and warm as possible; cover him with blankets or your coat to let his own body heat build up. Signs of shock are a rapid and weak pulse, glassy-eyed appearance, subnormal temperature, and slow capillary refill time. To determine the last

ymptom, press firmly against
he dog's gums until they turn
hite. Release and count the
umber of seconds until the
ums return to their normal
olor. If it is more than 2–3
econds, the dog may be going
to shock. Failure to return to
he reddish pink color indicates
hat the dog may be in serious
ouble and needs immediate
ssistance.

If artificial respiration is
equired, first open the dog's
outh and check for
bstructions; extend his tongue
nd examine the pharynx. Clear
s mouth of mucus and blood
nd hold the mouth slightly open.
outh-to-mouth resuscitation

involves holding the dog's
tongue to the bottom of his
mouth with one hand and sealing
his nostrils with the other while
you blow into his mouth. Watch
for his chest to rise with each
inflation. Repeat every 5–6
seconds, the equivalent of 10–12
breaths a minute.

If the veterinarian cannot
come to you, try to improvise a
stretcher to take the dog to him.

*To administer pills, simply press the
dog's lips against his teeth until he
opens his mouth. Then place the pill
as far back on the tongue as possible.
Now hold the dog's mouth closed and
see that the dog has swallowed.
Praise him for his cooperation.*

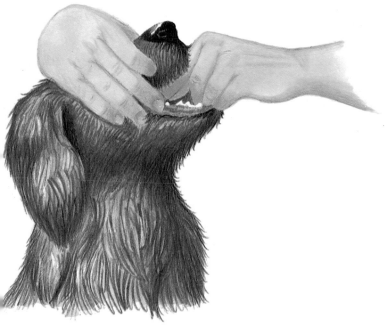

Health Care

To carry a puppy, wrap him in a blanket that has been folded into several thicknesses. If he is in shock, it is better to pick him up by holding one hand under his chest, the other under the hindquarters. This will keep him stretched out.

It is always better to roll an injured dog than to try and lift him. If you find him lying beside the road after a car accident, apply a muzzle even if you have to use someone's necktie to make one. Send someone for a blanket and roll him gently onto

Known as Elizabethan collars, these devices can be purchased at a pet store or provided by your veterinarian to prevent the dog from complications resulting from excessive licking or chewing.

it. Two people, one on each sid can make a stretcher out of th blanket and move the dog easi

If no blanket is available and the injured dog must be moved try to keep him as flat as possible. So many dogs' backs are broken in car accidents tha one must first consider that possibility. However, if he can move his hind legs or tail, his spine is probably not broken. G medical assistance for him immediately.

It should be mentioned that unfortunate car accidents, whi can maim or kill your dog, can avoided if he is confined at all times either indoors or, if out-c doors, in a fenced-in yard or

...ghtshade (left) and larkspur (right) are two plants that are poisonous when in-...sted. Many dogs eat small amounts of wild grass, which is often harmless if not ...rayed with pesticides; however, the owner must be cautious that poisonous plants ...e not growing in the grass, for they can be accidentally consumed.

...me other protective enclosure. ...ver allow your dog to roam ...e; even a well-trained dog ...ay, for some unknown reason, ...rt into the street—and the ...sult could be tragic.

...f you need to walk your dog, ...ash him first so that he will be ...otected from moving vehicles.

...OTECTING YOUR PET

...It is important to watch for any ...l-tale signs of illness so that ...u can spare your pet any ...necessary suffering. Your ...g's eyes, for example, should ...rmally be bright and alert, so if ...e haw is bloodshot or partially ...vers the eye, it may be a sign ...illness or irritation. If your dog ...s matter in the corners of his ...es, bathe them with a mild eye wash; obtain ointment or eye drops from your veterinarian to treat a chronic condition.

If your dog seems to have something wrong with his ears which causes him to scratch at them or shake his head, cautiously probe the ear with a cotton swab. An accumulation of wax will probably work itself out. Dirt or dried blood, however, is indicative of ear mites or infection and should be treated immediately. Sore ears in the summer, due to insect bites, should be washed with mild soap and water, then covered with a soothing ointment and wrapped in gauze if necessary. Keep your pet away from insects until his ears heal, even if this means confining him indoors.

Health Care

INOCULATIONS

Periodic check-ups by your veterinarian throughout your puppy's life are good health insurance. The person from whom your puppy was purchased should tell you what inoculations your puppy has had and when the next visit to the vet is necessary. You must make certain that your puppy has been vaccinated against the following infectious canine diseases: distemper, canine hepatitis, leptospirosis, rabies, parvovirus, and parainfluenza. Annual "boosters" thereafter provide inexpensive protection for your dog against such serious diseases. Puppies should also be checked for worms at an early age.

DISTEMPER

Young dogs are most susceptible to distemper, although it may affect dogs of all ages. Some signs of the disease are loss of appetite, depression, chills, and fever, as well as a watery discharge from the eyes and nose. Unless treated promptly, the disease goes into advanced stages with infections of the lungs, intestines, and nervous system. Dogs that recover may be impaired with paralysis, convulsions, a twitch, or some other defect, usually spastic in nature. Early inoculations in puppyhood

While the vet is inspecting your dog, secure him around the base of his neck and the tuck of his abdomen.

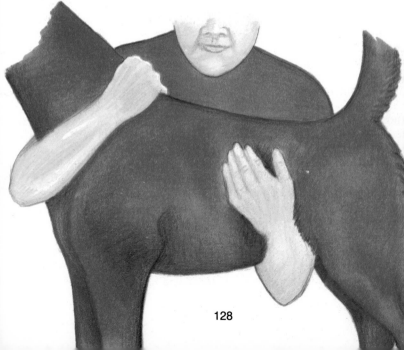

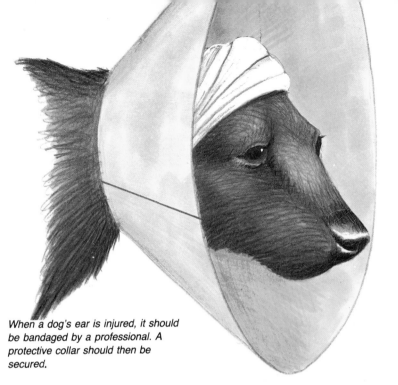

When a dog's ear is injured, it should be bandaged by a professional. A protective collar should then be secured.

should be followed by an annual booster to help protect against this disease.

CANINE HEPATITIS

The signs of hepatitis are drowsiness, vomiting, loss of appetite, high temperature, and great thirst. These signs may be accompanied by swellings of the head, neck, and abdomen. Vomiting may also occur. This disease strikes quickly, and death may occur in only a few hours. An annual booster shot is needed after the initial series of puppy shots.

LEPTOSPIROSIS

Infection caused by either of two serovars, *canicola* or *copehageni* is usually begun by the dog's licking substances contaminated by the urine or feces of infected animals. Brown rats are the main carriers of *copehageni*. The signs are weakness, vomiting, and a yellowish discoloration of the jaws, teeth, and tongue, caused by an inflammation of the kidneys. A veterinarian can administer the bacterins to protect your dog from this disease. The frequency of the doses is determined by the risk factor involved.

RABIES

This disease of the dog's central nervous system spreads by infectious saliva, which is transmitted by the bite of an infected animal. Of the two main classes of signs, the first is "furious rabies," in which the dog shows a period of melancholy or depression, then irritation, and finally paralysis. The first period can be from a few hours to several days, and during this time the dog is cross and will change his position often, lose his appetite, begin to lick, and bite or swallow foreign objects. During this phase the dog is spasmodically wild and has impulses to run away. The dog acts fearless and bites everything in sight. If he is caged or confined, he will fight at the bars and possibly break teeth or fracture his jaw. His bark becomes a peculiar howl. In the final stage, the animal's lower jaw becomes paralyzed and hangs down. He then walks with a stagger, and saliva drips from his mouth. About four to eight days after the onset of paralysis, the dog dies.

The second class of symptoms is referred to as "dumb rabies" and is characterized by the dog's walking in a bearlike manner with his head down. The lower jaw is paralyzed and the dog is unable to bite. It appears as if he has a bone caught in his throat.

If a dog is bitten by a rabid animal, he probably can be saved if he is taken to a veterinarian in time for a series of injections. After the signs appear, however, no cure is possible. The local health

Rats are the carriers of many diseases, including leptospirosis.

department must be notified in the case of a rabid dog, for he is a danger to all who come near him. As with the other shots each year, an annual rabies inoculation is very important. In many areas, the administration of rabies vaccines for dogs is required by law.

PARVOVIRUS

This relatively new virus is a contagious disease that has spread in almost epidemic proportions throughout certain sections of the United States. It has also appeared in Australia, Canada, and Europe. Canine parvovirus attacks the intestinal tract, white blood cells, and heart muscle. It is believed to spread through dog-to-dog contact, and the specific course of infection seems to come from fecal matter of infected dogs. Overcoming parvovirus is difficult, for it is capable of existing in the environment for many months under varying conditions and temperatures, and it can be transmitted from place to place on the hair and feet of infected dogs, as well as on the clothes and shoes of people.

Vomiting and severe diarrhea, which will appear within five to seven days after the animal has been exposed to the virus, are the initial signs of this disease. At the onset of illness, feces will be light gray or yellow-gray in

It is believed that mice can carry the early-stage deer ticks that may be carriers of the dreaded lyme disease.

color, and the urine might be blood-streaked. Because of the vomiting and severe diarrhea, the dog that has contracted the disease will dehydrate quickly. Depression and loss of appetite, as well as a rise in temperature, can accompany the other symptoms. Death caused by this disease usually occurs within 48 to 72 hours following the appearance of the symptoms. Puppies are hardest hit, and the virus is fatal to 75 percent of puppies that contract it. Death in

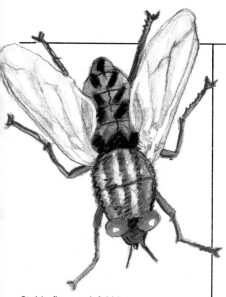

Stable fly: a painful bite.

puppies can be within two days of the onset of the illness.

A series of shots administered by a veterinarian is the best preventive measure for canine parvovirus. It is also important to disinfect the area where the dog is housed by using one part sodium hypochlorite solution (household bleach) to thirty parts of water and to keep the dog from coming into contact with the fecal matter of other dogs.

Deer tick: a carrier of lyme.

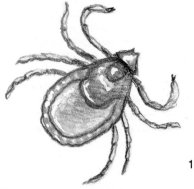

LYME DISEASE

Known as a bacterial infection, Lyme disease is transmitted by ticks infected with a spirochete known as *Borrelia burgdorferi*. The disease is most often acquired by the parasitic bite of an infected deer tick, *Ixodes dammini*. While the range of symptoms is broad, common warning signs include: rash beginning at the bite and soon extending in a bullseye-targetlike fashion; chills, fever, lack of balance, lethargy, and stiffness; swelling and pain, especially in the joints, possibly leading to arthritis or arthritic conditions; heart problems, weak limbs, facial paralysis, and lack of tactile sensation. Although there is no known cure-all, tetracycline and some other drugs have been prescribed with various degrees of success. If you suspect that your dog has Lyme disease, contact your vet immediately.

PARAINFLUENZA

Parainfluenza, or infectious canine tracheobronchitis, is commonly known as "kennel cough." It is highly contagious, affects the upper respiratory system, and is spread through direct or indirect contact with already diseased dogs. It will readily infect dogs of all ages that have not been vaccinated or that were previously infected. While this condition is definitely one of the serious diseases in dogs, it is self-limiting, usually lasting only two to four weeks. The symptoms are high fever and intense, harsh coughing that brings up mucus. As long as your pet sees your veterinarian immediately, the chances for his complete recovery are excellent.

EXTERNAL PARASITES

A parasite is an animal that lives in or on an organism of another species, known as the host, without contributing to the well-being of the host. The majority of dogs' skin problems are parasitic in nature and an estimated 90% of puppies are born with parasites.

Ticks can cause serious problems to dogs where the latter have access to woods, fields, and vegetation in which large numbers of native mammals live. Ticks are usually found clinging to vegetation and attach themselves to animals

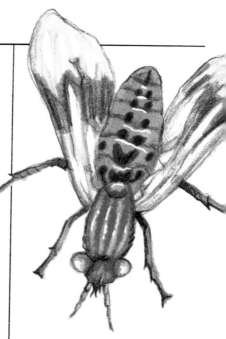

Deer fly: a welt-inducing bite.

passing by. They have eight legs and a heavy shield or shell-like covering on their upper surface. Only by keeping dogs away from tick-infested areas can ticks on dogs be prevented.

The flea is the single most common cause of skin and coat problems in dogs. There are 11,000 kinds of fleas which can transmit specific disorders like tapeworm and heartworm or transport smaller parasites onto your dog. The common tapeworm, for example, requires the flea as an intermediate host for completion of its life cycle.

A female flea can lay hundreds of eggs and these will become adults in less than three weeks. Depending on the temperature

Brown dog tick: a common parasite.

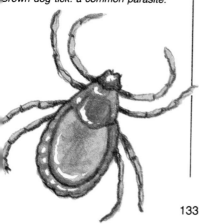

The bite of a single flea can cause an irritation that spreads quickly over the surface of the skin. For flea prevention, the dog and his living quarters should be treated regularly.

and the amount of moisture, large numbers of fleas can attack dogs. The ears of dogs, in particular, can play host to hundreds of fleas.

Fleas can lurk in crevices and cracks, carpets, and bedding for months, so frequent cleaning of your dog's environment is absolutely essential. If he is infected by other dogs, then have him bathed and "dipped," which means that he will be put into water containing a chemical that kills fleas. Your veterinarian will advise which dip to use, and your dog must be bathed for at least twenty minutes. These parasites are tenacious and remarkably agile creatures; fleas have existed since prehistoric times and have been found in arctic as well as tropical climates. Some experts claim that fleas can jump 150 times the length of their bodies; this makes them difficult to catch and kill. Thus, treating your pet for parasites without simultaneously

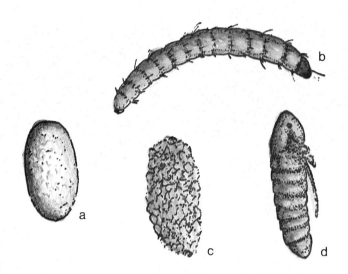

The life cycle of the flea: (a) egg (b) larvae (c) cocoon (d) pupae. If allowed to persist on the dog, fleas will build nests and reproduce, quickly infesting the dog. Regular brushing accompanied by anti-flea applications should suffice to eliminate the flea problem.

treating the environment is both inefficient and ineffective.

INTERNAL PARASITES

Four common internal parasites that may infect a dog are: roundworms, hookworms, whipworms, and tapeworms. The first three can be diagnosed by laboratory examination of the dog's stool, and tapeworms can be seen in the stool or attached to the hair around the anus. When a veterinarian determines what type of worm or worms are present, he then can advise the best treatment.

Roundworms, the dog's most common intestinal parasite, have a life cycle which permits complete eradication by worming twice, ten days apart. The first worming will remove all adults and the second will destroy all subsequently hatched eggs before they, in turn, can produce more parasites.

A dog in good physical condition is less susceptible to worm infestation than a weak dog. Proper sanitation and a nutritious diet help in preventing worms. One of the best preventive measures is to have clean, dry bedding for the dog, as this diminishes the possibility of reinfection due to flea or tick bites.

Health Care

Heartworm infestation in dogs is passed by mosquitoes. Dogs with this disease tire easily, have difficulty in breathing, and lose weight despite a hearty appetite. Administration of preventive medicine throughout the spring, summer, and fall months is advised. A veterinarian must first take a blood sample from the dog to test for the presence of the disease, and if the dog is heartworm-free, pills or liquid medicine can be prescribed.

Heartworm life cycle: a carrier mosquito bites a dog and deposits microfilariae; the filariae travel through the dog's blood stream, lodging in the heart to reproduce. The carrier dog is later bitten by an uninfected mosquito, which thereby acquires uninfectious microfilariae, develops the microfilariae to an infectious stage, bites and infects another dog.

CANINE SENIOR CITIZENS

The processes of aging and gradual degenerative changes start far earlier in a dog than often observed, usually at about seven years of age. If we recall that each year of a dog's life roughly corresponds to about seven years in the life of a man, by the age of seven he is well into middle age. Your pet will become less active, will have a poorer appetite with increased thirst, there will be frequent periods of constipation and less than normal passage of urine. His skin and coat might become dull and dry and his hair will become thin and fall out. There is a tendency towards obesity in old age, which should be avoided by maintaining a regular exercise program. Remember, also, that your pet will be less able to cope

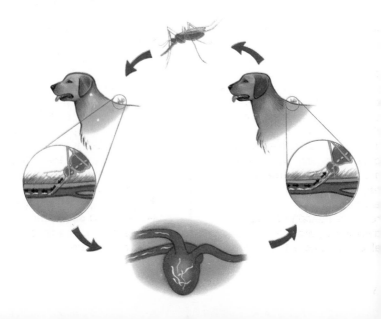

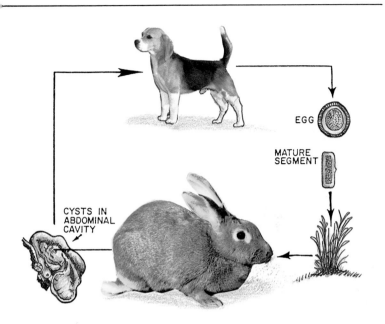

CYSTS IN
ABDOMINAL
CAVITY

EGG

MATURE
SEGMENT

Tapeworms can be acquired in a number of ways; the infected dog must receive veterinary treatment.

with extreme heat, cold, fatigue, and change in routine.

There is the possibility of loss or impairment of hearing or eyesight. He may become bad-tempered more often than in the past. Other ailments such as rheumatism, arthritis, kidney infections, heart disease, male prostatism, and hip dysplasia may occur. Of course, all these require a veterinarian's examination and recommendation of suitable treatment. Care of the teeth is also important in the aging dog.

Indeed, the mouth can be a barometer of nutritional health. Degenerating gums, heavy tartar on the teeth, loose teeth, and sore lips are common. The worst of all diseases in old age, however, is neglect. Good care in early life will have its effect on your dog's later years; the nutrition and general health care of his first few years can determine his lifespan and the quality of his life. It is worth bearing in mind that the older, compared to the younger, animal needs more protein of good biological value, more vitamins A, B-complex, D and E, more calcium and iron, less fat and fewer carbohydrates.

Preventive Dental Care

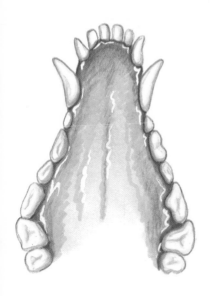 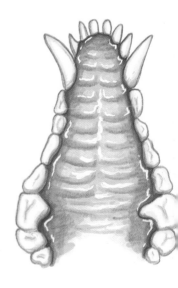

ALL DOGS NEED TO CHEW

Puppies and young dogs need something with resistance to chew on while their teeth and jaws are developing—to cut the puppy teeth, to induce growth of the permanent teeth under the puppy teeth, to assist in getting rid of the puppy teeth on time, to help the permanent teeth through the gums, to assure normal jaw development and to settle the permanent teeth solidly in the jaws.

The adult dog's desire to chew stems from the instinct for tooth cleaning, gum massage, and jaw exercise—plus the need to vent periodic doggie tensions. . . . A pacifier if you will!

Dental caries, as they affect the teeth of humans, are virtually

It is imperative that the owner take the necessary measures to ensure sound dental health. Ideal canine dentition illustrated: upper palate on right; lower palate on left.

unknown in dogs; but tartar (calculus) accumulates on the teeth of dogs, particularly at the gum line, more rapidly than on the teeth of humans. These accumulations, if not removed, bring irritation and then infection, which erode the tooth enamel and ultimately destroy the teeth at the roots. It is important that you take your dog to your local veterinarian for periodic dental examinations.

Tooth and jaw development will normally continue until the dog is more than a year old—but sometimes much longer, depending upon the dog, its chewing exercise, rate of calcium utilization and many other factors, known and unknown, which affect the development of individual dogs. Diseases, like distemper for example, may sometimes arrest development of the teeth and jaws, which may resume months or even years later.

This is why dogs, especially puppies and young dogs, will often destroy valuable property when their chewing instinct is not diverted from their owners'

his instinct tells him to chew. If your purposes, and those of your dog, are to be accomplished, what you provide for chewing must be desirable from the doggie viewpoint, have the necessary functional qualities, and, above all, be safe.

It is very important that dogs be prohibited from chewing on anything they can break or indigestible things from which they can bite sizeable chunks. Sharp pieces, such as those from a bone which can be broken by a dog, may pierce the intestinal wall and kill.

possessions, particularly during the widely varying critical period for young dogs. Saving your possessions from destruction, assuring proper development of teeth and jaws, providing for "interim" tooth cleaning and gum massage, and channeling doggie tensions into a non-destructive outlet are, therefore, all dependent upon the dog's having something suitable for chewing readily available when

A dog's teeth with little to no calculus build-up, a state achievable through consistent and appropriate care.

Indigestible things which can be bitten off in chunks, such as toys made of rubber compound or cheap plastic, may cause an intestinal stoppage; if not regurgitated, they are certain to bring painful death unless surgery is promptly performed.

NATURAL CHEW BONES

Strong natural bones, such as 4- to 8-inch lengths of round shin bone from mature beef—either the kind you can get from your butcher or one of the varieties available commercially in pet stores—may serve your dog's teething needs, if his mouth is large enough to handle them.

You may be tempted to give your puppy a smaller bone and he may not be able to break it when you do, but puppies grow rapidly and the power of their jaws constantly increases until maturity. This means that a growing dog may break one of the smaller bones at any time, swallow the pieces and die painfully before you realize what is wrong.

Many people have the mistaken notion that their dog's teeth are like those of wild carnivores or of dogs from antiquity. The teeth of wild carnivorous animals and those found in the fossils of the dog-like creatures of antiquity have far thicker and stronger enamel than those of our dogs today.

All hard natural bones are highly abrasive. If your dog is an avid chewer, natural bones may wear away his teeth prematurely; hence, they then should be taken away from your dog when the teething purposes have been served. The badly worn, and usually painful, teeth of many mature dogs can be traced to excessive chewing on animal bones. Contrary to popular belief, knuckle bones that can be chewed up and swallowed by the dog provide little, if any, useable calcium or other nutrient. They do, however, disturb the digestion of most dogs and might cause them to vomit the nourishing food they really need.

Never give a dog your old shoe to chew on, even if you have removed all the nails or metal parts, such as lace grommets, buckles, metal arches, and so on. Rubber heels are especially dangerous, as the dog can bite off chunks, swallow them, and suffer from intestinal blockage as a result. Additionally, if the rubber should happen to have a nail imbedded in it that you cannot detect, this could pierce or tear the intestinal wall. There is always the possibility, too, that your dog may fail to differentiate between his shoe and yours and chew up a good pair while you're not looking. It is strongly recommended that you refrain from offering old shoes as chew toys, since there are much safer products available.

RAWHIDE CHEWS

The most popular material from which dog chews are made is the hide from cows, horses, and other animals. Most of these chews are made in foreign countries where the quality of the hide is not good enough for

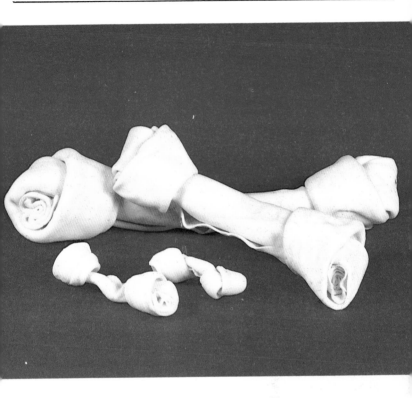

Many dogs love rawhide, and many stores carry a variety of rawhide chew products.

making leather. These foreign hides may contain lead, antibiotics, arsenic, or insecticides which might be detrimental to the health of your dog . . . or even your children. It is not impossible that a small child will start chewing on a piece of rawhide meant for the dog! Rawhide chews do not serve the primary chewing functions very well. They are also a bit messy when wet from mouthing, and most dogs chew them up rather rapidly. They have been considered safe for dogs until recently.

Rawhide is flavorful to dogs. They like it. Currently, some veterinarians have been attributing cases of acute constipation to large pieces of incompletely digested rawhide in ·the intestine. Basically it is good for them to chew on, but dogs think rawhide is food. They do not play with it nor do they use it as a pacifier to relieve doggie tension. They eat it as they would any other food. This is dangerous, for the hide is very difficult for dogs to digest and swallow, and many dogs choke on large particles of rawhide that become stuck in their throats. *Before you offer your dog rawhide chews, consult your veterinarian.* Vets have a lot of

Annealed nylon chews are recommended by veterinarians as proven-safe and effective canine chew devices.

experience with canine chewing devices; ask them what they recommend.

NYLON CHEW DEVICES

The nylon bones, especially those with natural meat and bone flavor added, are probably the most complete, safe, and economical answer to the chewing need. Dogs cannot break them nor bite off sizeable chunks; hence, they are completely safe. And being longer lasting than other things offered for the purpose, they are very economical.

Hard chewing raises little bristle-like projections on the surface of the nylon bones to provide effective interim tooth cleaning and vigorous gum massage, much in the same way your toothbrush does it for you. The little projections are raked off and swallowed in the form of thin shavings, but the chemistry of the nylon is such that they break down in the stomach fluids and pass through without effect.

The toughness of the nylon provides the strong chewing resistance needed for important jaw exercise and effective help for the teething functions; however, there is no tooth wear because nylon is non-abrasive. Being inert, nylon does not support the growth of microorganisms, and it can be washed in soap and water or sterilized by boiling or in an autoclave.

There are a great variety of Nylabone® products available that veterinarians recommend as safe and healthy for your dog or puppy to chew on. These Nylabone® Pooch Pacifiers® usually don't splinter, chip, or break off in large chunks; instead, they are frizzled by the

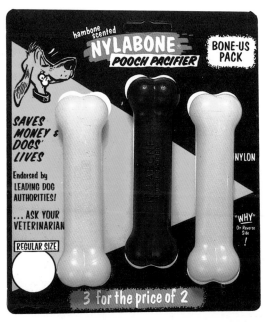

One of the many advantages of annealed nylon chew products is durability and long life. To keep your Nylabone® products sterile and to re-energize their flavor, these bones can be boiled in broth.

dog's chewing action, and this creates a toothbrush-like surface that cleanses the teeth and massages the gums. At the same time, these hard-nylon therapeutic devices channel doggie tension and chewing frustation into constructive rather than destructive behavior. The original nylon bone (Nylabone®) is not a toy and dogs use it only when in need of pacification. Keeping a bone in each of your dog's recreation rooms is the best method of

providing the requisite pacification. Unfortunately, many nylon chew products have been copied. These inferior quality copies are sold in supermarkets and other chain stores. The really good products are sold only through veterinarians, pet shops, grooming salons and places where the sales people really know something about dogs. The good products have the flavor impregnated *into* the bone. This makes the taste last longer. The smell is undetectable to humans. The artificial bones which have a strong odor are poor-quality bones with the odor sprayed on to impress the dog owner (not the dog)! These heavily scented dog toys may impart the odor to your carpets or furniture if an odor-sprayed bone lies there wet from a dog's chewing on it.

Food particles can be deposited between the teeth, where they are difficult to remove. Even the best chew products may not be able to free these decaying food pieces. For this reason, the Nylafloss® dental device is recommended. It is the only effective product to clean between the dog's teeth.

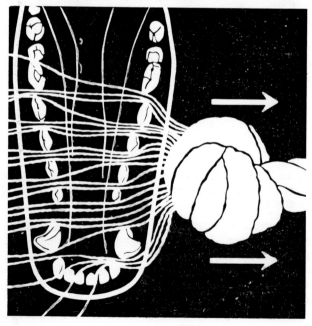

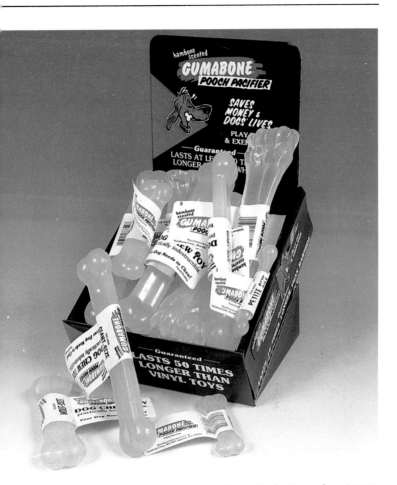

While satisfying the deep-rooted desire to chew, the dog's chewing a Gumabone® works to prevent tartar and plaque build-up. A dog should have access to an effective chew product at all times.

LOSS OR LOSS!

Most dentists relay that brushing daily is just not enough. In order to prevent unnecessary tooth loss, flossing is essential. For dogs, human dental floss is not the answer—however,

canine dental devices are available. The Nylafloss® is a revolutionary product that is designed to save dogs teeth and keep them healthy. Even though your dogs won't believe you, Nylafloss® is not a toy but rather

Prevention is the key to good dental health. It makes little sense to ignore your dog's dental needs; tooth problems can be costly and detrimental to your dog's well being. Nylafloss® is one very important part of preventive dental care.

a most effective agent in removing destructive plaque between the teeth and *beneath* the gum line where gum disease begins. Gentle tugging is all that is necessary to activate the Nylafloss®. These 100% inert nylon products are guaranteed to outlast rawhide chews by ten times and are available for sale at all pet shops.

THE IMPORTANCE OF PREVENTION

In order to get to the root of canine dentistry problems, it is important for owners to realize that no less than 75% of all canine dental health problems serious enough to require a vet's assistance and nearly 98% of all canine teeth lost are attributable to periodontal disease. Periodontal disease not only mars the teeth but also the gums and other buccal tissue in the mouth. Severe cases of periodontal disease involve resultant bacterial toxins which are absorbed into the blood stream and cause permanent damage to the heart and kidneys. In the infected mouth, teeth are loosened; tartar, unsightly and bad smelling, accumulates heavily; and the dog experiences a complete loss of appetite. Long-standing periodontitis can also manifest itself in simple symptoms such

diarrhea and vomiting.
Periodontal disease deserves the attention of every dog owner—a dog's teeth are extremely important to his ongoing health. The accumulation of plaque, food matter mixed with saliva attaching itself to the tooth surface, is a sure sign of potential bacteria build-up. As toxic material gathers, the bone surrounding the teeth erodes. If plaque and calculus continue to reside without attention, bacteria-fighting cells will form residual pus at the root of the teeth, dividing the gum from the tooth. The debris is toxic and actually kills the buccal tissue. This is a most undesirable situation, as hardened dental calculus is one of the most direct causative agents of periodontitis.

In actuality, the disease is a result of a number of contributing factors. Old age, a diet comprised solely of soft or semi-soft foods, dental tartar, constant chewing of hair and even coprophagy (the eating of stool) are among the most common contributors.

Just as regular dental visits and brushing are necessary for humans, regular hygienic care and veterinary check-ups can help control tooth problems in canines. Involved and expensive routines can be performed on the affected, neglected mouth and teeth if decay has begun

eroding the enamel and infecting the gums. Cleaning, polishing, and scaling are routine to remove calculus build-up.

Owners must claim responsibility for their dog's health, and tooth care is no small aspect of the care required. Daily brushing with a salt/baking soda solution is the best answer, but many owners find this tedious or just too difficult to perform. The simpler and more proven effective way to avoid, reduce, and fight periodontal disease and calculus build-up is giving the dog regular access to a thermoplastic polymer chew device. The Gumabone® products are the only scientifically proven line that offers the desired protection from calculus and tartar build-up.

CANINE DENTAL BREAKTHROUGH

The independent research of Dr. Andrew Duke, D.V.M., reveals that 70% of the dogs that regularly use Gumabone® experience a reduction of calculus build-up. This find is a breakthrough for the dog world, since the Gumabone® has already resided in the toy boxes of many dogs as their favorite play item. Little did owners know previously that their dogs were gaining entertainment and unparalleled dental treatment at the same time. Dr. Duke writes: "There is little debate left that

THE CALCULUS INDEX

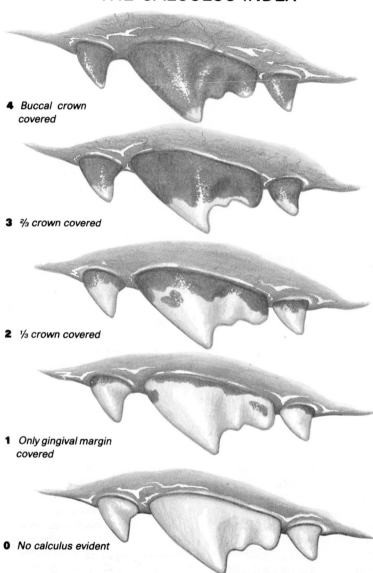

4 *Buccal crown covered*

3 *⅔ crown covered*

2 *⅓ crown covered*

1 *Only gingival margin covered*

0 *No calculus evident*

*An artist's representation of the calculus index, ranging from index rating **4** (topmost drawing) through index rating **0** (lowest drawing).*

dental calculus is an excellent indicator of periodontal health in the dog, just as it is in humans. "Calculus does not cause gingivitis and periodontitis, but the plaque and bacteria that cause periodontitis are responsible for the mineral precipitation we know as 'calculus.' All veterinarians who have made a study of dogs' oral

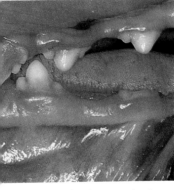

A dog's teeth showing a moderate calculus build-up.

health have noticed the middle aged dog who actively chews with excellent gingival health. Many of these dogs that chew hard substances regularly wear the cusps down and even may expose the pulp cavity faster than secondary dentin can be formed. Often these 'excellent chewers' are presented with slab fractures of the premolars

or apical abcesses.

"The challenge then becomes to find a substance which is effective in removing calculus and plaque but does not wear the enamel excessively. In an attempt to duplicate the chewstuffs enjoyed by dogs in the wild, researchers have used bovine tracheas to demonstrate the inhibition of plaque and gingivitis. Very little else has been done in veterinary medicine to establish a scientific basis for evaluating chewstuffs.

"In the human field it is generally accepted (incorrectly) that fibrous foodstuffs and diet have no effect on oral health. This is a moot point since the practice of brushing is by far a more efficient technique of preventing plaque accumulation, calculus and periodontal disease. Studies in human subjects failed to find any benefits in eating apples, raw carrots, etc. If people are not allowed to brush, it is difficult to conduct clinical trials of more than one week.

"The increased awareness of animals' dental health of recent years has resulted in most veterinary practitioners' recommending some kind of chewstuff to their dog owners. To meet this market demand, there has been a stampede into the market by vendors ready to promote their products. The veterinarian is furnished no

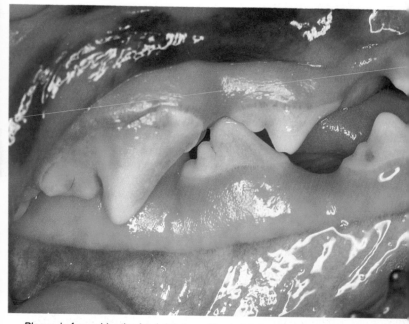

Plaque is formed by the food debris and bacterial deposits on the teeth. Due to the high carbon dioxide and pH level in the mouth, minerals precipitate on the plaque to form calculus.

scientific data, but is asked to promote rawhide, bounce, and squeaky toys. How would our human colleagues handle this situation? Can Listerine® say that it prevents colds, but not support the claim? Can Tartar Control Crest® or Colgate Tartar Control Formula® be sold if it is not proven that it does in fact reduce tartar? Of course not.

"To this end, the following study was made.

"*Method:* Twenty dogs of different breeds and age were selected from a veterinary practice's clientele. Although most were from multiple pet households, none were colony dogs. The owners were asked if they would allow their dogs to be anesthetized for two prophylactic cleanings which included root planing, polishing, and gingival debridement necessary to insure good oral hygiene.

"The dogs were divided into two groups of 10. Their teeth were cleaned and their calculus

ndex converted to 0. One group
was allowed only their normal
dry commercial dog ration for 30
days. The other was allowed to
have free choice access to
Gumabone® products of the
appropriate size.

"After 30 days, photoslides
were made of the upper 3rd
premolar, upper 4th premolar,
and the lower 4th premolar on
both sides of the dog's mouth.
The dogs were again subjected
to a prophylactic cleaning and
the group reversed. After the
second 30 days, photoslides
were again made. A total of six
teeth in each mouth were
evaluated on each dog. This was
80 slides representing 240
teeth."

Fourteen out of 20 dogs (or
70%) experienced a reduction in
calculus build-up by regularly

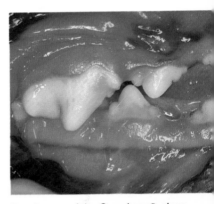

*Regular use of the Gumabone® chew
products can significantly reduce
plaque build-up.*

using the Gumabone® product.
These products are available in a
variety of sizes (for different size
dogs) and designed in
interesting shapes: bones, balls,
knots and rings (and even a tug
toy). The entertainment value of
the Gumabone® products is but
an added advantage to the
fighting of tooth decay and
periodontitis. The products are
ham-flavored and made of a
thermoplastic polymer that is
designed to outlast by ten times
any other rawhide, rubber or
vinyl chew product, none of
which can promise the proven
benefit of the Gumabone®.

If your dog is able to chew
apart a Gumabone®, it is
probable that you provided him
with a bone that is too small for
him. Replace it with a larger one
and the problem should not re-

*Teeth of affected canine showing little
to no plaque or calculus build-up after
professional cleaning.*

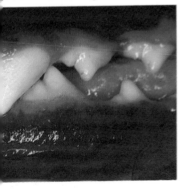

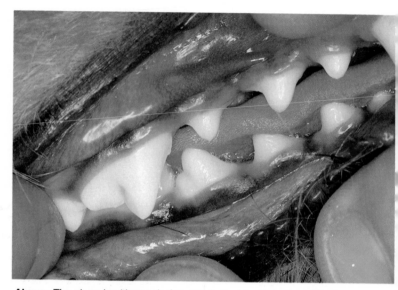

Above: The clean healthy teeth that are desired in dogs should inspire owners to work towards better dental hygiene. *Below:* The beginning of undesirable deposits forming on improperly maintained teeth.

materialize. Economically, the Gumabone® is a smart choice, even without comparing it to the cost of extensive dental care.

Of course, nothing can *substitute* for periodic professional attention to your dog's teeth and gums, no more than your toothbrush can replace your dentist. Have your dog's teeth cleaned by your veterinarian at least once a year—twice a year is better—and he will be healthier, happier, and a far more pleasant companion.

Gumabones® are available through veterinarians and pet shops.

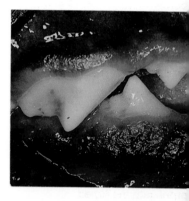

Breeding

If you own a bitch and you want to breed her, first make sure you can handle the responsibility of caring for her and her litter of pups. Consider the time and money involved just to get her into breeding condition and then to sustain her throughout pregnancy and afterwards while she tends her young. You will be obligated to house, feed, groom, and housebreak the puppies until good homes can be found for them; and, lest we forget, there will be periodic trips to the vet for check-ups, wormings, and inoculations. Common sense should tell you that it is indeed cruel to bring unwanted or unplanned puppies into an already crowded canine world; only negligent pet owners allow this to happen. With pet-quality purebred dogs, most breeders require prospective pet owners to sign a neuter/spay agreement when they purchase their dogs. In this way breeders can be assured that only their very best stock of show-quality and breeder-quality animals, i.e., those that match closely their individual standards of perfection and those that are free of genetic disorders or disease, will be used to propagate the breed.

Before you select a stud to mate with your bitch, think carefully about why you want her to give birth to a litter of puppies. If you feel she will be deprived in some way if she is not bred, if you think your children will learn from the experience, if you have the mistaken notion that you will make money from this great undertaking, think again. A dog can lead a perfectly happy, healthy, normal life without having been mated; in fact, spaying a female and neutering a male helps them become better pets, as they are not so anxious to search for a mate in an effort to relieve their sexual tensions. As for giving the children a lesson in sex education, this is hardly a valid reason for breeding your dog. And on an economic level, it takes not only years of hard work (researching pedigrees and bloodlines, studying genetics, among other things), but it takes plenty of capital (money, equipment, facilities) to make a decent profit from dog breeding. Why most dedicated breeders are lucky just to break even. If you have only a casual interest in dog breeding, it is best to leave this pastime to those who are more experienced in such matters, those who consider it a serious hobby or vocation. If you have bought a breeder– or show-quality canine, one that may be capable of producing champions, and if you are just starting out with this breeding venture, seek advice from the seller of your dog, from other veteran breeders, and from your vet before you begin.

Breeding

THE FEMALE "IN SEASON"

A bitch may come into season (also known as "heat" or estrus) once or several times a year, depending on the particular breed and the individual dog. Her first seasonal period, that is to say, the time when she is capable of being fertilized by a male dog, may occur as early as six months with some breeds. If you own a female and your portion of the female's reproductive tract; the soft, flabby vulva indicates her readiness to mate. Around this second week or so ovulation occurs, and this is the crucial period for her to be bred, if this is what you have in mind for her. It is during this middle phase of the heat cycle when conception can take place. Just remember that there is great variation from

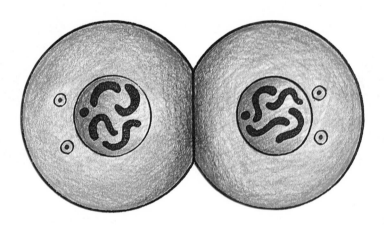

Cells reproduce by a process called mitosis, in which the cells divide, forming two identical cells.

intention is *not* to breed her, by all means discuss with the vet the possibility of having her spayed: this means before she reaches sexual maturity.

The first sign of the female's being in season is a thin red discharge, which may increase for about a week; it then changes color to a thin yellowish stain, which lasts about another week. Simultaneously, there is a swelling of the vulva, the exterior bitch to bitch with regard to how often they come into heat, how long the heat cycles last, how long the period of ovulation lasts, and how much time elapses between heat cycles. Generally, after the third week of heat, the vulval swelling decreases and the estrus period

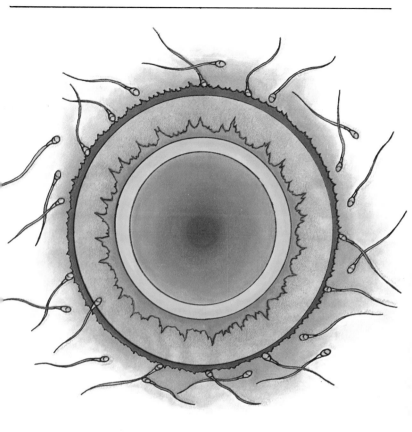

ceases for several months.

It should be mentioned that the female will probably lose her puppy coat, or at least shed part of it, about three months after she has come into season. This is the time when her puppies would have been weaned, had she been mated, and females generally drop coat at this time.

With female dogs, there are few, if any, behavioral changes during estrus. A bitch may dart out of an open door to greet all

The egg within the female is surrounded by a wall that normally takes many sperm to penetrate. In this way, only the strongest sperm will fertilize the egg. A fertile female in season usually has a number of eggs, known as gametes.

available male dogs that show an interest in her, and she may occasionally raise her tail and assume a mating stance, particularly if you pet her lower back; but these signs are not as

Breeding

dramatic as those of the sexually mature male. He himself does not experience heat cycles; rather, he is attracted to the female during all phases of her seasonal period. He usually becomes more aggressive and tends to fight with other males, especially over females in heat. He tends to mark his territory with urine to attract females and at the same time to warn other competitive males. It is not uncommon to see him mount various objects, and people, in an effort to satisfy his mature sexual urges.

If you are a homeowner and you have an absolutely climb-proof and dig-proof run within your yard, it may be safe to leave your bitch in season there. But then again it may not be a wise idea, as there have been cases of males mating with females right through chain-link fencing! Just to be on the safe side, shut her indoors during her heat periods and don't let her outdoors until you are certain the estrus period is over. Never leave a bitch in heat outdoors, unsupervised, even for a minute so that she can defecate or

A whelping box provides the female with a safe place to deliver her pups. Introduce the female to the box several days prior to delivery to get her adjusted to it. Later, when whelping is near, move her to the box so that she may prepare for delivery.

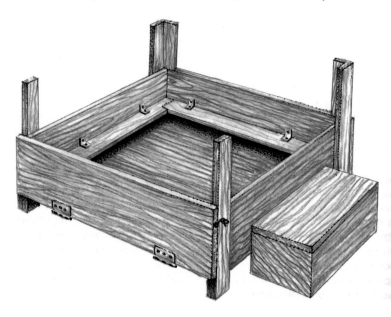

156

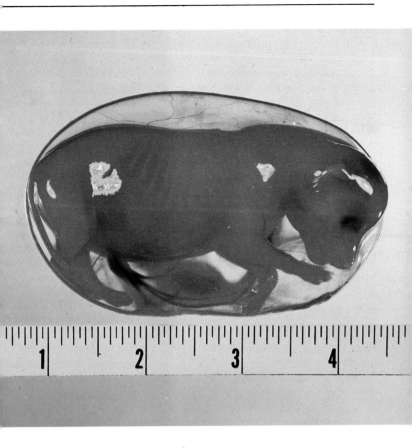

While in the womb, each pup is encased within a protective sac.

inate. If you want to prevent
e neighborhood dogs from
anging around your doorstep,
s they inevitably will do when
ey discover your female is in
eason, take her some distance
way from the house before you
t her do her business.
therwise, these canine suitors
ill be attracted to her by the
rousing odor of her urine, and
ey will know instinctively that
he isn't far from her scented

"calling card." If you need to
walk your bitch, take her in the
car to a nearby park or field for a
chance to stretch her legs.
Remember that after about three
weeks, and this varies from dog
to dog, you can let her outdoors
again with no worry that she can
have puppies until the next heat
period.

Breeding

WHEN TO BREED

It is usually best to breed a bitch when she comes into her second or third season. Plan in advance the time of year which is best for you, taking into account your own schedule of activities (vacations, business trips, social engagements, and so on). Make sure you will be able to set aside plenty of time to assist with whelping of the newborn pups and caring for the dam and her litter for the next few weeks. At the very least, it probably will take an hour or so each day just to feed and clean up after the brood—but undoubtedly you will find it takes much longer if you stop to admire and play with the youngsters periodically! Refrain from selling the litter until it is at least six weeks old, keeping in mind that a litter of pups takes up a fair amount of space by then. It will be your responsibility to provide for them until they have been weaned from their mother, properly socialized, housebroken, and ready to go to new homes (unless you plan to keep them all). Hopefully, as strongly recommended, you will have already lined up buyers for the pups in advance of their arrival into this world.

CHOOSING THE STUD

You can plan to breed your female about six-and-one-half months after the start of her last season, although a variation of a month or two either way is not unusual. Do some research int the various bloodlines within your breed and then choose a stud dog and make arrangements well in advance. you are breeding for show stoc which will command higher prices than pet-quality animals, mate should be chosen very carefully. He should compleme any deficiencies (bad traits) tha your female may have, and he should have a good show reco or be the sire of show winners, he is old enough to have prove himself. If possible, the bitch an stud should have several ancestors in common within th last two or three generations, a such combinations have been known, generally, to "click" bes

The owner of a stud dog usually charges a stud fee for use of the animal's services. Th does not always guarantee a litter, but if she fails to conceiv chances are you may be able t breed your female to that stud

Facing page: Dogs have an averag gestation period of 63 to 65 days. Th chart gives the expected delivery da according to the date on which th bitch was mated. The due date is a approximation only, and the own should be prepared well in advance the due date, especially with first-tim mothers. If a bitch is mated more tha once, the owner should use the date the first mating but realize th possibility of a later deliver

PERPETUAL WHELPING CHART

Bred / Due	Day-by-day chart (bred day → whelping day)
Bred—Jan.	1 2 3 4 5 6 7 8 9 10 11 12 13 14 15 16 17 18 19 20 21 22 23 24 25 26 27 28 29 30 31
Due—March	5 6 7 8 9 10 11 12 13 14 15 16 17 18 19 20 21 22 23 24 25 26 27 28 29 30 31 **April** 1 2 3 4
Bred—Feb.	1 2 3 4 5 6 7 8 9 10 11 12 13 14 15 16 17 18 19 20 21 22 23 24 25 26 27 28
Due—April	5 6 7 8 9 10 11 12 13 14 15 16 17 18 19 20 21 22 23 24 25 26 27 28 29 30 **May** 1 2
Bred—Mar.	1 2 3 4 5 6 7 8 9 10 11 12 13 14 15 16 17 18 19 20 21 22 23 24 25 26 27 28 29 30 31
Due—May	3 4 5 6 7 8 9 10 11 12 13 14 15 16 17 18 19 20 21 22 23 24 25 26 27 28 29 30 31 **June** 1 2
Bred—Apr.	1 2 3 4 5 6 7 8 9 10 11 12 13 14 15 16 17 18 19 20 21 22 23 24 25 26 27 28 29 30
Due—June	3 4 5 6 7 8 9 10 11 12 13 14 15 16 17 18 19 20 21 22 23 24 25 26 27 28 29 30 **July** 1 2
Bred—May	1 2 3 4 5 6 7 8 9 10 11 12 13 14 15 16 17 18 19 20 21 22 23 24 25 26 27 28 29 30 31
Due—July	3 4 5 6 7 8 9 10 11 12 13 14 15 16 17 18 19 20 21 22 23 24 25 26 27 28 29 30 31 **August** 1 2
Bred—June	1 2 3 4 5 6 7 8 9 10 11 12 13 14 15 16 17 18 19 20 21 22 23 24 25 26 27 28 29 30
Due—Aug.	3 4 5 6 7 8 9 10 11 12 13 14 15 16 17 18 19 20 21 22 23 24 25 26 27 28 29 30 31 **Sept.** 1
Bred—July	1 2 3 4 5 6 7 8 9 10 11 12 13 14 15 16 17 18 19 20 21 22 23 24 25 26 27 28 29 30 31
Due—September	2 3 4 5 6 7 8 9 10 11 12 13 14 15 16 17 18 19 20 21 22 23 24 25 26 27 28 29 30 **Oct.** 1 2
Bred—Aug.	1 2 3 4 5 6 7 8 9 10 11 12 13 14 15 16 17 18 19 20 21 22 23 24 25 26 27 28 29 30 31
Due—October	3 4 5 6 7 8 9 10 11 12 13 14 15 16 17 18 19 20 21 22 23 24 25 26 27 28 29 30 31 **Nov.** 1 2
Bred—Sept.	1 2 3 4 5 6 7 8 9 10 11 12 13 14 15 16 17 18 19 20 21 22 23 24 25 26 27 28 29 30
Due—November	3 4 5 6 7 8 9 10 11 12 13 14 15 16 17 18 19 20 21 22 23 24 25 26 27 28 29 30 **Dec.** 1 2
Bred—Oct.	1 2 3 4 5 6 7 8 9 10 11 12 13 14 15 16 17 18 19 20 21 22 23 24 25 26 27 28 29 30 31
Due—December	3 4 5 6 7 8 9 10 11 12 13 14 15 16 17 18 19 20 21 22 23 24 25 26 27 28 29 30 31 **Jan.** 1 2
Bred—Nov.	1 2 3 4 5 6 7 8 9 10 11 12 13 14 15 16 17 18 19 20 21 22 23 24 25 26 27 28 29 30
Due—January	3 4 5 6 7 8 9 10 11 12 13 14 15 16 17 18 19 20 21 22 23 24 25 26 27 28 29 30 31 **Feb.** 1
Bred—Dec.	1 2 3 4 5 6 7 8 9 10 11 12 13 14 15 16 17 18 19 20 21 22 23 24 25 26 27 28 29 30 31
Due—February	2 3 4 5 6 7 8 9 10 11 12 13 14 15 16 17 18 19 20 21 22 23 24 25 26 27 28 **March** 1 2 3 4

again. In some instances the owner of the stud will agree to take a "first pick of the litter" in place of a fee. You should, of course, settle all details beforehand, including the possibility of a single puppy surviving, deciding the age at which the pup is to be taken, and so forth.

If you plan to raise a litter that will be sold exclusively as pets,

The reproductive system of the female dog consists of a highly specialized group of organs situated at the rear of the animal.

and if you merely plan to make use of an available male (not a top stud dog), the most important selection point involves temperament. Make sure the dog is friendly, as well as healthy, because a bad disposition can be passed on to his puppies—and this is the worst of all traits in a dog destined to be a pet. If you are breeding pet-quality dogs, a "stud fee puppy," not necessarily the choice of the litter, is the usual payment. Don

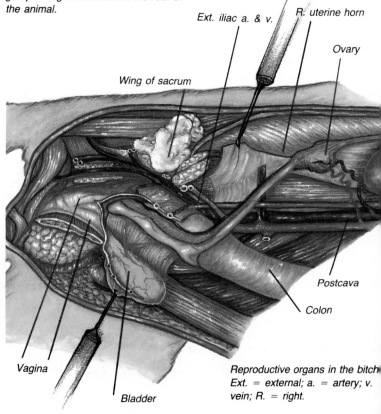

Ext. iliac a. & v.

R. uterine horn

Ovary

Wing of sacrum

Postcava

Colon

Vagina

Bladder

Reproductive organs in the bitch
Ext. = external; a. = artery; v. = vein; R. = right.

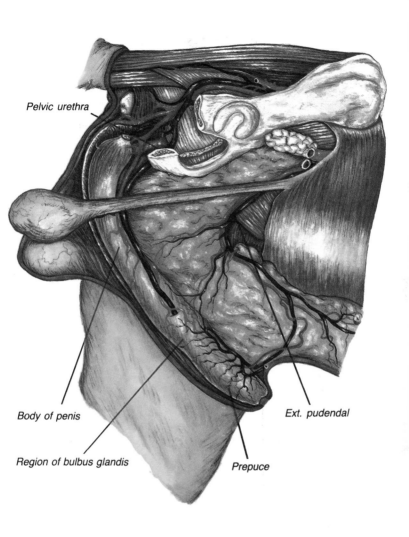

Pelvic urethra

Body of penis

Region of bulbus glandis

Ext. pudendal

Prepuce

The reproductive system of the male dog includes the penis and testicles. The sperm and testosterone producing testes are contained within the scrotal sac. When not excited, the penis is withdrawn into the dog. The dog's penis is unique in that the base of the shaft has a bulbous swelling that forbids retraction from the vagina until some time has passed after intercourse.

breed indiscriminately; be sure you will be able to find good homes for each of the pups, or be sure you have the facilities to keep them yourself, *before* you plan to mate your dog.

PREPARATION FOR BREEDING

Before you breed your female, make sure she is in good health.

Breeding

She should be neither too thin nor too fat. Any skin disease *must* be cured first so that it is not passed on to the puppies. If she has worms, she should be wormed before being bred or within three weeks after the mating. It is generally considered a good idea to revaccinate her against distemper and hepatitis before the puppies are born. This will increase the immunity the puppies receive during their early, most vulnerable period.

The female will probably be ready to breed twelve days after the first colored discharge appears. You can usually make arrangements to board her with the owner of the stud for a few days, to insure her being there at the proper time; or you can take her to be mated and bring her home the same day if you live near enough to the stud's owner. If the bitch still appears receptive she may be bred again two days later, just to make certain the mating was successful. However, some females never show signs of willingness, so it helps to have an experienced breeder on hand. In fact, you both may have to assist with the

The canine uterus is quite different from the human uterus. Besides the difference in shape, the canine uterus is designed to house an average of five to eight offspring.

OVARY

HORN OF UTERUS

BLADDER —

BODY OF UTERUS

CANINE UTERUS
Before mating

VAGINA

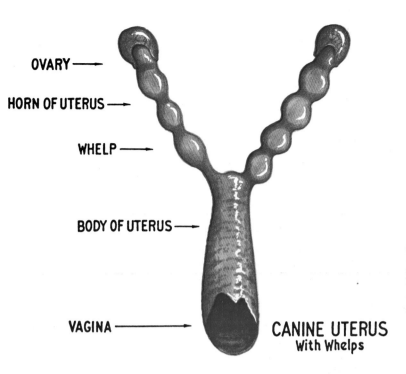

OVARY

HORN OF UTERUS

WHELP

BODY OF UTERUS

VAGINA

CANINE UTERUS
With Whelps

Prior to birth, the developing pups are housed in the horns of the uterus.

mating by holding the animals against each other to ensure the "tie" is not broken, that is, to make certain copulation takes place. Sometimes, too, you'll need to muzzle the bitch to keep her from biting you or the stud.

Usually the second day after the discharge changes color is the proper time to mate the bitch, and she may be bred for about three days following this time. For an additional week or so, she may have some discharge and attract other dogs by her odor; but she should not be bred. Once she has been bred, keep her far from all other

male dogs, as they have the capacity to impregnate her again and sire some of her puppies. This could prove disastrous where purebred puppies—especially show-quality ones—are concerned.

THE FEMALE IN WHELP

You can expect the puppies nine weeks from the day of the mating, although sixty-one days is as common as sixty-three. Gestation, that period when the pups are developing inside their mother, varies among individual bitches. During this time the female should receive normal

Breeding

care and exercise. If she was overweight at the start, don't increase her food right away; excess weight at whelping time can be a problem with some dogs. If she is on the thin side, however, supplement her meal or meals with a portion of milk and biscuit at noontime. This will help build her up and put weight on her.

You may want to add a mineral and vitamin supplement to her diet, on the advice of your veterinarian, since she will need an extra supply not only for herself but for the puppies growing inside of her. As the mother's appetite increases, feed her more. During the last two weeks of pregnancy, the pups grow enormously and the mother will have little room for food and less of an appetite. She should be tempted with meat, liver, and milk, however.

As the female in whelp grows heavier, cut out violent exercise

Using simple genetic rules, an owner can predict to some degree the traits that the offspring of a given mating can exhibit. The six possible ways in which a pair of determiners can unite are illustrated on this Mendelian expectation chart. Ratios apply to expectancy over large numbers, except in lines 1, 2, and 6 where exact expectancy is realized in every litter.

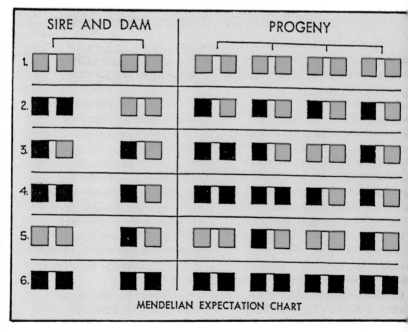

MENDELIAN EXPECTATION CHART

d jumping from her usual
utine. Although a dog used to
ch activities will often play with
e children or run around
luntarily, restrain her for her
vn sake.

A sign that whelping is
minent is the loss of hair
ound her breasts. This is
ture's way of "clearing a
th" so that the puppies will be
le to find their source of
urishment. As parturition
aws near, the breasts will have
elled with milk and the nipples
Il have enlarged and darkened
a rosy pink. If the hair in the
east region does not shed for
me reason, you can easily cut
short with a pair of scissors or
mb it out so that it does not
at and become a hindrance to
e suckling pups later on.

EPARING FOR THE PUPPIES

Prepare a whelping box a few
ys before the puppies are due,
d allow the mother to sleep
ere overnight or to spend
me time in it during the day to
come accustomed to it. This
y she is less likely to try to
ve her pups under the front
rch or in the middle of your
d. A variety of places will
rve, such as the corner of your
llar or garage (provided these
ces are warm and dry). An
used room, such as a dimly lit
are bedroom, can also serve
the place for delivery. If the
ather is warm, a large outdoor

dog house will do, as long as it is
well protected from rain, drafts,
and the cold—and enclosed by
fencing or a run. A whelping box
serves to separate mother and
puppies from visitors and other
distractions. The walls should be
high enough to restrain the
puppies yet low enough to allow
the mother to take a short
respite from her brood after she
has fed them. Four feet square is
minimum size (for most dogs)
and six-to-eight-inch high walls
will keep the pups in until they
begin to climb; then side walls
should be built up so that the
young ones cannot wander away
from their nest. As the puppies
grow, they really need more
room anyway, so double the
space with a very low partition
down the middle of the box, and
soon you will find them naturally
housebreaking themselves.
Puppies rarely relieve
themselves where they sleep.
Layers of newspapers spread
over the whole area will make
excellent bedding and be
absorbent enough to keep the
surface warm and dry. These
should be removed daily and
replaced with another thick layer.
An old quilt or washable blanket
makes better footing for the
nursing puppies than slippery
newspaper during the first week;
this is also softer for the mother
to lie on.

Be prepared for the actual
whelping several days in

Breeding

advance. Usually the mother will tear up papers, refuse food, and become restless. These may be false alarms; the real test is her temperature, which will drop to below 100°F (38°C) about twelve hours before whelping. Take her temperature with a rectal thermometer, morning and evening, and usher her to her whelping box when her temperature goes down. Keep a close watch on her and make sure she stays safely indoors (or outdoors in a safe enclosure); if she is let outside, unleashed, or allowed to roam freely, she could wander off and start to go into labor. It is possible that she could whelp anywhere, and this could be unfortunate if she needs your assistance.

WHELPING

Usually little help is needed from you, but it is wise to stay close to be sure that the mother's lack of experience (if this is her first time) does not cause an unnecessary complication. Be ready to help when the first puppy arrives, for it could smother if she does not break the amniotic membrane enclosing it. She should tear open the sac and start licking the puppy, drying and stimulating it. Check to see that all fluids have been cleared from the pup's nostrils and mouth after the mother has licked her youngster clean; otherwise the pup may

have difficulty breathing. If the mother fails to tear open the s and stimulate the newborn's breathing, you can do this yourself by tearing the sack wi your hands and then gently rubbing the infant with a soft, rough towel. The afterbirth attached to the puppy by the long umbilical cord should follow the birth of each puppy. Watch to be sure that each afterbirth is expelled, for the retention of this material can cause infection. In her instinct for cleanliness the mother will probably eat the afterbirth afte severing the umbilical cord. On or two meals of this will not hu her; they stimulate her milk supply, as well as labor, for remaining pups. However, eati too many afterbirths can make her lose appetite for the food she needs to feed her pups an regain her strength. So remove the rest of them, along with th wet newspapers, and keep the box dry and clean.

If the mother does not bite t cord or bites it too close to th puppy's body, take over the jo to prevent an umbilical hernia. Tearing is recommended, but you can cut the cord, about tw inches from the body, with a sawing motion with scissors th have been sterilized in alcohol. Then dip the end of the cut co in a shallow dish of iodine; the cord will dry up and fall off in a few days.

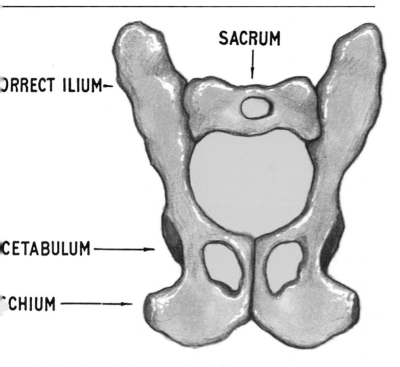

SACRUM

CORRECT ILIUM—

ACETABULUM ——→

ISCHIUM ——→

Shape of pelvic entrance in the average female dog, showing adequate aperture through which the whelps have to pass.

The puppies should follow each other at intervals of not more than half an hour. If more than one goes past and you are sure there are still pups to come, taking the mother for a brisk walk outside may start labor again. If she is actively straining without producing a puppy, the youngster may be presented backward, a so-called "breech" birth. Careful assistance with a well-lubricated finger to feel for the puppy or to ease it back may help, but never attempt to pull it

out by force. This could cause serious damage, so seek the services of an expert—your veterinarian or an experienced breeder.

Even the best planned breeding can bear unexpected problems and complications. Therefore, do not rely solely on textbook knowledge of breeding and genetics. Experienced breeders and veterinarians will generally lend their words of wisdom—take full advantage of their generosity. Mere trial and error is no basis for any responsible breeding program.

If *anything* seems wrong during labor or parturition, waste no time in calling your veterinarian, who will examine the bitch and, if necessary, give her hormones to stimulate the birth of the remaining puppies. You may want his experience in whelping the litter even if all goes well. He will probably prefer to have the puppies born at his hospital rather than getting up in the middle of the night to come

A puppy nurser kit is considered standard equipment by many breeders. These kits are available at your local pet shop.

to your home. The mother wou no doubt, prefer to stay at hom but you can be sure she will g the best of care in a veterinary hospital. If the puppies are bo at home, and all goes as it should, watch the mother carefully afterward. Within a da or two of the birth, it is wise to have the veterinarian check he and the pups to ensure that all well.

Be sure each puppy finds a teat and starts nursing right away, as these first few meals supply colostral antibodies to help him fight disease. As soo as he is dry, hold each puppy a nipple for a good meal witho competition. Then he may join his littermates in the whelping box, out of his mother's way while she continues giving birt Keep a supply of puppy formu on hand for emergency feedin or later weaning. An alternativ formula of evaporated milk, co syrup, and a little water with e yolk can be warmed and fed if necessary. A pet nurser kit is also a good thing to have on hand; these are available at lo pet shops. A supplementary feeding often helps weak pups (those that may have difficulty nursing) over the hump. Keep track of birth weights and wee readings thereafter; this will furnish an accurate record of t pups' growth and health, and t information will be valuable to your veterinarian.

RAISING THE PUPPIES

After all the puppies have been born, take the mother outside for a walk and drink of water, and then return her to take care of her brood. She will probably not want to stay away for more than a minute or two for the first few weeks. Be sure to keep water available at all times and feed her milk or broth frequently, as she needs nourishment to produce milk. Encourage her to eat, with her favorite foods, until she seeks them of her own accord. She will soon develop a ravenous appetite and should have at least two large meals a day, with dry food available in addition. Your veterinarian can guide you on the finer points of nutrition as they apply to nursing dams.

Prepare a warm place to put the puppies after they are born to keep them dry and to help them to a good start in life. An electric heating pad, heat lamp or hot water bottle covered with flannel can be placed in the bottom of a cardboard box and near the mother so that she can see her puppies. She will usually allow you to help her care for the youngsters, but don't take them out of her sight. Let her handle things if your interference seems to make her nervous.

Be sure that all the puppies are getting enough to eat. If the mother sits or stands instead of lying still to nurse, the probable cause is scratching from the puppies' nails. You can remedy this by clipping them, as you would the bitch's, with a pet nail clipper. Manicure scissors also do for these tiny claws. Some breeders advise disposing of the smaller or weaker pups in a large litter, as the mother has trouble handling more than six or seven. You can help her out by preparing an extra puppy box or basket furnished with a heating pad and/or heating lamp and some bedding material. Leave half the litter with the mother and the other half in the extra box, changing off at two-hour intervals at first. Later you may exchange them less frequently, leaving them all together except during the day. Try supplementary feedings, too. As soon as their eyes open, at about two weeks, they will lap from a small dish.

WEANING THE PUPPIES

Normally the puppies should be completely weaned at five weeks, although you can start to feed them at three weeks. They will find it easier to lap semi-solid food than to drink milk at first, so mix baby cereal with whole or evaporated milk, warmed to body temperature, and offer it to the puppies in a saucer. Until they learn to lap it, it is best to feed one or two at a time because they are more likely to walk into it than to eat it. Hold the saucer at their chin level, and let them gather around, keeping paws off

Breeding

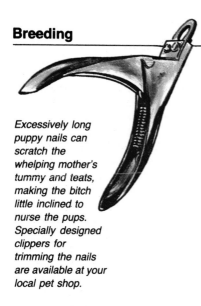

Excessively long puppy nails can scratch the whelping mother's tummy and teats, making the bitch little inclined to nurse the pups. Specially designed clippers for trimming the nails are available at your local pet shop.

the dish. Cleaning with a damp sponge afterward prevents most of the cereal from sticking to the pups if the mother doesn't clean them up. Once they have gotten the idea, broth or babies' meat soup may be alternated with milk, and you can start them on finely chopped meat. At about four weeks, they will eat four meals a day and soon do without their mother entirely. Start them on canned dog food, or leave dry puppy food with them in a dish for self-feeding. Don't leave the water dish with them all the time; at this age everything is a play toy and they will use it as a wading pool. They can drink all they need if it is offered several times a day, after meals. As the puppies grow up, the mother will go into their "pen" only to nurse them, first sitting up and then standing. To dry up her milk

supply completely, keep the mother away for longer periods; after a few days of part-time nursing she can stay away for even longer periods, and then permanently. The little milk left will be resorbed by her body.

The puppies may be put outside during the day, unless it is too cold or rainy, as soon as their eyes are open. They will benefit from the sunlight. A rubber mat or newspapers underneath will protect them from cold or dampness. As they mature, the pups can be let out for longer intervals, although you must provide them with a shelter at night or in bad weather. By now, cleaning up after the matured youngsters is a man-sized job, so put them out at least during the day and make your task easier. If you enclose them in a run or kennel, remember to clean it *daily*, as various parasites and other infectious organisms may be lurking if the quarters are kept dirty.

You can expect the pups to need at least one worming before they are ready to go to new homes. Before the pups are three weeks old, take a stool sample from each to your veterinarian. The vet can determine, by analyzing the stool, if any of the pups have worms—and if so, what kind of worms are present. If one puppy is infected, then all should be

ormed as a preventive
measure. Follow the
veterinarian's advice; this also
applies to vaccinations. You will
want to vaccinate the pups at the
earliest possible age. This way,
the pups destined for new
homes will be protected against
some of the more debilitating
canine diseases.

THE DECISION TO SPAY OR NEUTER

If you decide not to use your
male or female for breeding, or if
you are obligated to have the
animal altered based on an
agreement made between you
and the seller, make the
necessary arrangements with
your veterinarian as soon as
possible. The surgery involved
for both males and females is
relatively simple and painless:
males will be castrated and
females will have their ovaries
and uterus removed. In both
cases, the operation does not
alter their personalities; you will,
however, notice that males will
be less likely to roam, to get into
fights with other male dogs, and
to mount objects and people.

Your veterinarian can best
determine at what age neutering
or spaying should be done. With
a young female dog, the
operation may be somewhat
more involved, and as a result be
more costly; however, in the long
run you will be glad you made
the decision to have this done
for your pet. After a night or two
at the veterinarian's or an animal
hospital, your bitch can be safely
returned to your home. Her
stitches will heal in a short time,
and when they are removed, you
will hardly notice her souvenir
scar of the routine operation.
Once she has been spayed, she
no longer will be capable of
having a litter of puppies.
Pet adoption agencies and
other animal welfare
organizations can house only so
many animals at one time, given
the money, space, and other
resources they have available.
This is why pet owners are urged
to have their pets altered, so that
puppies resulting from
accidental breedings won't end
up being put to sleep as so many
others have that are lost, stray,
unwanted, or abandoned.

op view of a dog's skeletal structure. The dog is a highly specialized animal.

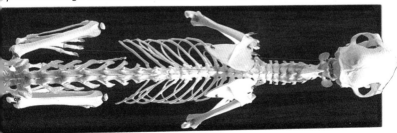

Dogs and the Law

By Anmarie Barrie, Esq.

This chapter is written merely as a general survey of the laws pertaining to dogs. The laws vary tremendously from jurisdiction to jurisdiction. They also change over time, and are subject to the interpretation of the controlling authorities.

Any reference to a resource material or facility is not an endorsement.

As civilization advances and living conditions become more crowded, laws are created to keep society functioning smoothly. Our lives become more regulated. This includes how we care for our dogs.

Laws dealing with dogs are in effect at all levels of government. Mostly, though, dog law is a local affair. There are many dog laws. They vary from country to country and from city to city. However, there are general rules and guidelines that are common to all dog laws.

BUYING AND SELLING

Most of the law regulating buyers, sellers, and breeders of dogs pertains to dealers. A dealer is a person who buys and sells dogs in the regular course of his business. Therefore, an owner who sells the family pet's puppies at a yard sale is not covered. However, some laws do encompass the occasional seller.

If you regularly sell, keep, or breed more than a certain number of dogs, you may need kennel or breeder's license. Puppies may or may not be included in this number. Usually diseased dogs, and dogs under specified age, are forbidden to be sold.

Whether you are the buyer or the seller, put the sales agreement in writing. Until you write it out, you may not realize that you and the other party have different understandings. The agreement should include, but certainly not limited to, the following:

1. Breed, sex, age, color, quality, and birth date of the dog
2. Names and addresses of

172

the buyer and the seller

3. Name and address of the breeder

4. Names and registration numbers of the sire and dam (pedigree)

5. Date of the last veterinary exam, the name and address of the veterinarian, and any findings

6. Date and types of vaccinations

7. Behavior (viciousness) and propensities (training) of the dog

8. Any health problems the dog may have

9. Any warranties (guarantees) the seller is making

10. The name of the original owner (if the seller purchased the dog from someone else).

GENERAL GUIDELINES FOR DOG OWNERS

Licenses

Probably wherever you live, a dog needs a license. A license involves a fee and usually has to be renewed periodically. It should be worn by the dog at all times. Puppies under a certain age are exempt from the licensing requirements. A license may cost less for a spayed or neutered dog, an assistance dog, or a dog belonging to an old or disabled person. To find out where to get a license, talk to your pet shop owner, veterinarian, local officials, the animal control or health department, or look in the telephone book.

Licensed and unlicensed dogs may be accorded different treatment under the law. Any unlicensed dog, or a dog running at large without a license tag, may be impounded. Unlicensed dogs that are impounded are destroyed or sold sooner than licensed dogs, because local authorities are unable to trace ownership. Furthermore, some authorities permit the killing of an unlicensed dog, or a licensed dog not wearing its license, at any given time. Yet a dog wearing a license can be killed only if it is attacking a person or livestock.

Dogs and the Law

If your dog is lost or stolen, it will be harder to find if it does not have a license. An owner of an unlicensed dog may be subject to a fine or penalty.

Vaccinations

A current rabies vaccination is a common requirement. Other inoculations, such as a distemper shot, may be necessary as well. Proof of vaccination may be required in order to get a license. Puppies under a certain age are not required to be vaccinated.

Leash Laws

Many areas have leash laws. These laws require a dog to be under the control of its owner at all times. This may involve confinement, that the dog be on a leash, or even muzzled.

No dog should be allowed to roam free. A dog at large could be impounded and disposed of according to regulations. Its owner may be fined and have to pay for the cost of confining the dog. Some communities have special areas where dogs are allowed to run loose.

Other Restrictions

Muzzle laws are becoming more popular, as are laws requiring owners to clean up their dog's solid waste (pooper-scooper laws) if deposited anywhere off their own property. Many buildings, such as restaurants, apartments, and hotels, and other areas, such as beaches, are strictly off limits to dogs. Owners of assistance dogs are commonly excluded from these laws.

You should also be aware that some municipalities actually prohibit a dog from being left alone in a car. An owner may be violating anti-cruelty laws.

How Many Dogs Allowed?

Many animal lovers have more than one dog. However, some communities restrict the number of dogs allowed per household, and some residencies refuse to permit dogs at all.

These laws are taken quite seriously. If your condominium or apartment lease has a no-pets clause, you can be evicted for harboring a dog. If your residence limits the number of dogs you can keep, exceeding that number can subject you to a daily fine.

If you want to keep more dogs, you may need to apply for a city permit or a kennel license. This may entail extra fees, rules, and inspections.

An owner may be required to dispose of the number of dogs exceeding the allowable limit. Fines and jail sentences can be imposed as well. These enforcement measures can be imposed even if you are caring for someone else's dog only temporarily. Puppies less than a certain age may or may not be exempted.

Lost and Found

If your dog is lost, call any agency you think handles dogs. Include the police, health and animal control departments, and humane societies. Listen to local radio stations and read the local newspapers that list found animals. Visit the police station, animal shelter, and government offices where lists may be posted. Leave a picture and an accurate description of the dog every place you visit. If at first you are not successful, keep asking around. The dog may show up later.

If you find a dog, attempt to find its owner, or give the dog to the local authorities. If you do not make an effort to return the dog to its owner, you may be liable to the owner for the value of the dog. The law may require you to notify the animal control authorities.

If the dog remains in your possession, check for

Dogs and the Law

identification. The dog may have the name and address of its owner on a tag. Call the owner. If the dog has a license tag, call the agency that issued the tag to get the name of the owner.

Ask local residents if they recognize the dog. Post signs around the area where the dog was found. Put a notice in the paper and notify the local radio station.

Impoundment laws often give animal control officials the authority to pick up, impound, sell, and/or destroy dogs. However, since a dog is considered the personal property of its owner, a dog cannot be confiscated without notice, and possibly a hearing.

An owner's property rights may be lost, though, under certain conditions. Any unlicensed dog, or a dog running at large without a vaccination tag, or running at large without a license tag may be impounded without first notifying its owner.

Dogs running around loose are

pical pound inhabitants. jured, abandoned, and vicious ogs also end up at the pound. A og that has bitten a person, aused damage, or been eclared a nuisance can be aken from its owner and npounded. An owner who has s dog in his possession, ough, is entitled to be notified efore the dog is seized. An wner must usually be notified gain before the dog is estroyed.

A pound is required to keep ie dog for a prescribed period f time before it can take action. the owner can be identified, he iust be notified. To reclaim the og, an owner may have to have ie dog licensed, vaccinated, pay fine, and pay a charge for every ay that the dog is kept. If the wner does not claim the dog, it an be sold, offered for doption, or killed in a humane ianner. The law may allow a dog o be given to an assistance dog gency or a research facility.

Dog laws may be enforced by ny number of agencies. These iclude the police, a humane ociety, an animal control center, r a health department. No iatter which organization is responsible for enforcing the law, all of them must respect the legal rights of an owner.

Burial

Contact your local animal control authority for information on how to dispose of your dog's remains. You may not be permitted to bury the dog on your own property. You may have to bring the dog's body to a pet cemetery. The wisest thing to do is to have your vet handle the burial. Some towns will dispose of the dog for a fee.

DOGS AS PROPERTY

A dog is personal property. This fact has a lot of legal implications, because an owner of property has legally enforceable rights. The law prohibits a person from injuring, taking, or destroying the property of another. So an owner who has a property interest in

Dogs and the Law

his dog is entitled to compensation if his dog is killed, stolen, or injured.

Damages typically include actual out-of-pocket expenses. But other criteria may have some bearing as well. For example, consider the market value and age of the dog. Its type, traits, pedigree, and purchase price are all legitimate concerns. The feelings of the owner will probably not be considered in a damage award. Other considerations include registration, breeding value, value as a watchdog, and if the dog is expecting a litter.

For an owner to enforce his rights as an owner of property, the dog may need to be licensed. An owner of an unlicensed dog may not be afforded any protection under the law. An owner of a puppy that does not yet require a license should still benefit from the property laws concerning dogs.

Since a dog is not a person, it cannot be a beneficiary of a will. It cannot inherit money or other property. If you want your dog to

cared for after your death,
you must designate a new owner
for the dog in your will. It is wise
to leave money to the new owner
to care for your dog. Be sure to
consider medical expenses—as
your dog gets older, its
veterinary bills will increase.

A dog may be contested
property in a divorce proceeding.
A court will determine custody
and visitation rights.

Property cannot be taken from
an owner without due process of
the law. This means that the dog
owner must have notice, and
possibly be given a hearing
before his property is taken or
destroyed. Therefore, before a
dog can be impounded, killed, or
offered for adoption, its owner
must be given adequate notice.
The amount of time considered
"adequate notice" varies from
place to place and may depend
on whether or not the dog is
licensed.

Who is Responsible for the Dog?

An owner is legally responsible
for controlling his dog. However,
the definition of an owner may
be broad enough to include the
legal owner, as well as anyone
who cares for, harbors, or has
custody of the dog. So someone
besides the owner, or more than
one person, may be liable for the
actions of the dog.

A dog owner may be a minor.
In such a situation, the
youngster's parents or legal
guardian may be responsible for
any injury or damage caused by
the dog. Under certain
circumstances, a landlord may
be responsible. The landlord
must have known that a tenant's
dog was dangerous, have had

the power to remove the dog, but did nothing about it.

A veterinarian and his staff members may be injured by a dog during the course of its treatment. The dog owner is probably not responsible because these people know and accept the risk of injury. Of course, an owner cannot conceal the fact that his dog is dangerous. A doctor has insurance to cover these mishaps.

Liability for Damage and Injury

Typically, an owner is legally liable for any personal injury or property damage (including killing livestock) caused by his pet. Depending upon the circumstances, an owner may fined or jailed as well.

An owner may have to pay medical expenses. This can include costs for doctors, hospitals, medications, physical therapy, and counselling. A victim may also be entitled to compensation for loss of earnings if he was out of work due to his injury. The time off may involve both treatment and recuperation.

Some victims of dog attacks are awarded compensation for pain and suffering. The amount

of the award can vary tremendously depending on the circumstances because it is difficult to calculate the cost specifically. Sometimes a spouse or close relative can receive compensation as well. The theory is loss of service of the injured person. Loss of service is not limited to economics; it may also include loss of companionship.

If the fault on the part of the owner is particularly shocking or reckless, an award may be doubled or even tripled. Additionally, the victim may be entitled to punitive damages. This recovery punishes the owner's poor conduct by making him pay even more than the amount considered adequate compensation to the victim. The financial status of the owner can be taken into account when establishing a punitive damage award.

Also, the owner will have to take measures designed to prevent further detriment. In serious cases, this could mean destruction of the dog. Since any dog can cause injury or damage under the right circumstances, a prudent owner will take precautionary measures designed to prevent his dog from causing harm.

There are several legal theories under which dog owners may be found liable for their dog's acts. Some of the

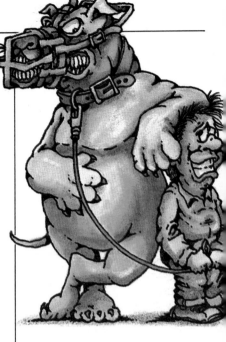

theories are strict liability, common law rules, negligence, and nuisance. Strict liability means that the owner is responsible for the dog's actions even though the owner is not at fault in any way. Common law doctrines are defined in court decisions. They are not codified in statutes. An owner is negligent if he does not exercise reasonable and ordinary care in controlling his dog. A dog is a nuisance if it unreasonably and substantially offends or inconveniences a person.

Often there is an on-duty exemption for trained police or military dogs. The police or government may be immune from liability if the injury occurred because the dog was

Dogs and the Law

provoked or while it was working.

Vicious Dogs

Once a dog has bitten or exhibited menacing behavior, it may be officially declared a vicious dog. Dogs that have been trained to attack or fight may also be considered vicious. A few dog breeds are believed to be inherently dangerous.

Owners of such vicious dogs may be required to take further measures to control their dogs. The dogs may have to be securely confined at all times, on a leash and muzzled when in public, and have a special vicious dog license. The dog may have to be tattooed. The owner may be required to have liability insurance for the dog. Signs may be necessary to warn the public that a vicious dog is in residence. A bond may have to be posted with the municipality to cover any potential injury or damage. Some cities ban vicious dogs.

An owner who fails to comply with the law may be fined or jailed. He may also be liable for double or triple the amount of damage caused by the dog. The dog may be impounded and killed.

Preventing Injury

If you are a dog owner or keeper, the best way to avoid liability is to prevent injury. Adhere to a few common sense rules to keep risk of harm to a minimum.

No matter how small, old or timid the dog is, it can hurt someone, damage property, or be a nuisance. Any dog may bite or scratch if it is threatened, or if it is protecting its owner, its puppies, or its food. A dog racing around a corner or barking unexpectedly may startle an unsuspecting person and result in injury.

Therefore, keep your dog securely contained in the house or yard. Be sure it cannot escape to scare or otherwise get in the way of strangers. Post warning signs that alert passers-by that a dog is present. Never let your dog off its leash to run at large. The owner must be in control at all times.

Lastly, keep the dog's license and vaccinations up-to-date. If your dog does manage to get free, its return will be more expedient if it is properly identified. The less time out of your care, the less time the dog has to cause trouble. Should the dog bite someone, the dog will not need to be quarantined if its rabies vaccine is current.

Dogs and the Law

Insurance

The cost of the potential damage and injury inflicted by a dog can be enormous. A wise owner will check to see that his homeowner's or renter's policy covers his dog. A dog that has a menacing behavior should have its own insurance coverage. Dangerous and vicious dogs may be obligated by law to have liability insurance.

A typical homeowner's or renter's insurance plan covers any damage caused by the policy holder's negligence. This coverage often extends to incidents that take place away from the owner's property, even if a vehicle is involved. If policy does not extend to vehicular events, look to your auto insurance plan. Some insurance companies refuse to issue a policy altogether if a vicious dog lives in the home.

Often a plan limits its coverage to the first instance of harm caused by a dog. After that, the owner must pay out of his own pocket. Other companies exclude certain types of dog-related harm from their coverage. This is why it is important to read your policy carefully. If you do not understand the terms, call your agent for an explanation. It is important to know your liability before an accident occurs.

If your home and auto insurance do not extend to dog-related injuries, or you think the coverage is not broad enough, buy insurance for your pet. Take out insurance that will protect you and the dog while at home and/or away.

Your dog may become ill or injured. Get coverage that will pay for its medical expenses. Some insurance firms offer pet health insurance. These policies may pay for medications, doctors' bills, and hospital fees.

Handling a Controversy

A dog can be dangerous, or it can be just a nuisance. Either way, if you have a dog like this in your neighborhood, or if it is your dog, you may be involved in a dispute. Your dog may have caused injury or damage, or your dog may have been the victim. Either way, you should be prepared to handle the controversy in a responsible and legally acceptable manner.

A dog may not be dangerous, but it can be a nuisance. Some irksome antics include digging up a yard, chasing a car, scattering garbage across the lawn, ravaging a prized garden, barking incessantly, roaming the neighborhood, and frightening people.

If you are the property owner, the first thing to do is to talk to the owner of the dog. Use a reasonable and friendly approach—*avoid animosity*. Offer your neighbor some advice

as to how to stop the dog's bad habits. Suggest obedience school or calling the local humane society for some tips. If the dog's poor behavior stops, call on your neighbor again to thank him for taking the necessary measures.

If you happen to be the owner of the dog wreaking havoc, be understanding, not hostile. After all, you are responsible for keeping your dog from annoying your neighbors. Your neighbor has probably had several encounters with your dog before he came to talk to you. Take the proper measures to stop the

dog's poor behavior. After a few days, visit your neighbor to be sure the problem has been solved.

If talking to your neighbor is a dead-end, try mediation. This method of settling disputes outside of a courtroom involves the imposition of a neutral third party. This individual acts as a link between the disputing parties to keep the lines of communication open. A mediator does not choose sides, he merely identifies problems and suggests compromises. Once the differences are settled, define the terms in a writing

Dogs and the Law

signed by both parties.

There may be a reason that you do not want to talk to your neighbor, or talking to him proves disastrous, or maybe you just do not know who owns the troublesome dog. Call your police, animal control department, health or public safety authorities. The people responsible for controlling dogs can call or visit the dog owner, or even issue a citation.

Look up all the pertinent local law, such as ordinances dealing with noise, vicious dogs, leash laws, nuisances, dogs running at large, personal injury, property damage, or the number of dogs allowed per household, and have it enforced. Enlist the aid of other neighbors who are annoyed. And, most importantly, be persistent.

You may be compelled to go to court. If so, familiarize yourself with the law so that you can make sure your complaint meets all the required elements. Good preparation is vital to presenting a sound argument. Be brief and articulate, not boring. Present your case in an organized manner. You may be allowed to present witnesses, and to utilize documents, police reports, hospital records, medical bills, and photographs. Avoid

confusion or repetition. But most importantly, always be respectful to both the judge and your adversary.

CRUELTY

In most modern societies, cruelty against dogs is forbidden. Inhumane treatment may include intentional abuse, neglect, theft, abandonment, and dog fighting. Cropping ears and tails without using anesthesia, leaving a dog which was hit by your car, confining a dog in a parked car, and poor conditions in a shelter may all be considered cruelty. In Great Britain, ear cropping is expressly prohibited. It is lawful, though, to kill a dog in the act of injuring a person or damaging property. Using dogs for scientific research is usually not punishable by law, even though it is distasteful.

If you suspect improper behavior, first talk to the owner. If the maltreatment does not cease, report the abuse to the humane society, the police, a local dog society, or anyone else you think has the right to take action. It is best to have the complaint in writing. Keep a copy for yourself.

Except in the case of an emergency, the dog owner is entitled to notice before his dog can be taken away. A mistreated dog is seized by the authorities and impounded. If the cruelty is particularly outrageous, the abuser may be subject to a fine or a jail sentence.

TRAVEL

It is a common sight to see a

dog owner traveling with his pet. In fact, many owners refuse to go anywhere without their dog. However, most owners do not realize that traveling is stressful for their pet. So if you are not going to leave your dog at home, at least make the trip as comfortable as possible.

Restrictions regarding pet travel are constantly changing due to health and international situations. Therefore, call the appropriate agricultural department, embassy, or consulate before departing. Most countries require a recent certificate of health. Vaccinations may be necessary.

Of course, your dog should be properly identified. A tag with the dog's name, and your name, address, and phone number should be attached to the dog at all times.

Each container should be plainly marked, labeled, or tagged on the outside with the names and addresses of the shipper and the consignee. An accurate invoice statement specifying the number of each species contained in the shipment must also be included.

Since the hours of service and the availability of inspectors vary from port to port, check with your anticipated port of arrival prior to importation. This will reduce the possibility of unnecessary delay.

An airline may refuse to transport an animal unless specific criteria are met. Common restrictions include that the dog must be at least eight weeks old; certified as

althy; secured in a carrier; and dequately identified.

A dog traveling on an airline ust be contained in a shipping ate. The crate should be sturdy ad well ventilated. It should be rge enough to allow your pet to and, turn around, and lie down omfortably. The carrier should e marked *"Live Animals"* and *This End Up."* Your name, ddress, and phone number, the g's name, and the destination ould be on the crate.

ANDLORDS AND DOGS

Many landlords prefer not to nt to dog owners. A dog can sturb other tenants if it is isy, messy, or smelly. Under e right circumstances, any dog can destroy property or injure a person. A landlord can experience a lot of aggravation and expense. Violation of an existing no-pets clause may be a sufficient cause for eviction or a penalty.

A no-dogs policy may be negotiable. An exception may be made if the prospective tenant can assure the landlord that the dog will not be a problem. But how do you convince the landlord?

There are several things that can be done. Introduce the dog to the landlord. The landlord can see for himself that the dog is well groomed and well mannered. An untrained puppy is not as desirable as a mature, adult dog. A spayed or neutered dog will probably get bonus points. Bring along written references from previous landlords and neighbors saying that the dog has not been a problem and is well liked.

Special provisions can be negotiated in private leases that are fair to both sides. Dog owners are still responsible for damage and injury caused by their dogs.

Index

Required Reading

The Atlas of Dog Breeds of the World By Bonnie Wilcox, DVM, & Chris Walkowicz (H-1091)
Traces the history and highlights the characteristics, appearance and function of every recognized dog breed in the world. 409 different breeds receive full-color treatment and individual study. Hundreds of breeds in addition to those recognized by the American Kennel Club and the Kennel Club of Great Britain are included—the dogs of the world complete! The ultimate reference work, comprehensive coverage, intelligent and delightful discussions. The perfect gift book. *Hard cover, 9 × 12", 912 pages, 1,106 color photos. ISBN 0-86622-930-2*

Dog Training By Lew Burke (H-962)
The elements of dog training are easy to grasp and apply. The author uses the psychological makeup of dogs to his advantage by making them want to be what they should be—substituting the family for the pack. *Hard cover, 5½" × 8", 255 pages, 64 black and white photos, 23 color photos. ISBN 0-87666-656-X*

The Complete Dog Buyer's Guide By Dr. William Bruette & Kerry V. Donnelly (H-989)
Plots the advances in veterinary care and genetics of the last fifty years by incorporating descriptions of the breeds as they are today. Many of the photos illustrate Best In Show winners and top and historical dogs. Individual complete sections on breeding, selection, caring, etc. *Hard cover, 5½" × 8", 608 pages. Illustrated ISBN 0-86622-026-7*

The Mini Atlas of Dog Breeds By Andrew De Prisco & James B. Johnson (H-1106)
An identification handbook giving a concise and thorough look at over 400 of the world's dog breeds. The authors' enthusiastic and knowledgeable approach brings to life instantly man's oldest friend and companion. A flowing and witty text, further enlivened by 500 full-color photos, successfully maps out the world of dogs; an easy-reference format pinpoints each breed's development, portrait, registry, and pet attributes. The volume is captioned with specially designed symbols. *Hard cover, 5½" × 8½", 544 pages, nearly 700 color photos. ISBN 0-86622-091-7*

Dog Owner's Encyclopedia of Veterinary Medicine By Allan H. Hart B.V.Sc. (H-934)
Written by a vet who feels that most dog owners should recognize the symptoms and understand the cures of most diseases of dogs so they can properly communicate with their veterinarian. This book is a necessity for every dog owner, especially those who have more than one dog. *Hard cover, 5½" × 8", 186 pages, 88 black and white photos. ISBN 0-87666-287-4*

Dog Breeding for Professionals By Dr. Herbert Richards (H-969)
For dog owners who need and actively seek good advice about how to go about breeding their dogs whether for profit or purely because of their attachment to animals. *Please note* that the breeding photography is sexually explicit and some readers may find it offensive. *Hard cover, 5½" × 8", 224 pages, 105 black and white photos, 62 color photos. ISBN 0-87666-659-4*

Dogs and the Law By Anmarie Barrie, Esq. (DS-130)
A practical and reliable survey of laws pertaining to our dogs. Advice concerning liability, licenses, impound, vehicles, insurance, wills, vaccinations and many other useful and often entertaining topics. Full color cartoon illustrations add a delightful twist. *Hard cover, 6" × 9", 160 pages, over 55 color illustrations, appendices, charts. ISBN 0-86622-088-7*